Juv
Bio
Judah

...s from the West

DATE DUE			
JAN 1 2 1991			
NOV 4 1991			
1-31-92			
JAN 9 1992			
JAN 0 6 1998			
MAY 2 7 1998			

GAYLORD M-2   PRINTED IN U.S.A.

RCE.

D0788275

THEODORE DEHONE JUDAH

RAILS FROM THE WEST

...A BIOGRAPHY OF THEODORE D. JUDAH

By Helen Hinckley Jones

Golden West Books

San Marino, California

Golden West Books

P.O. BOX 8136 • SAN MARINO, CALIFORNIA • 91108

Introduction

THE BUILDING OF THE Pacific Railway one hundred years ago was one of the greatest enterprises in American history. In three short years of actual construction some 20,000 Americans graded, built track, and affixed the steel for 1,800 miles of railroad. Reaching out ever westward — over the Great Plains, the Rocky Mountains, the Great Basin, and the rugged mountains of California — the Pacific Railroad connected Chicago, St. Louis, and all points east with the Pacific Coast.

No man did more to bring to pass this colossal and daring enterprise than the young American engineer, Theodore Judah. Idealistic and yet practical, energetic and yet with the vision that comes from contemplating the future, Theodore Judah is a native hero worth reading about.

From the time men had begun to dream of binding the nation together with bands of steel, it had been recognized that the most difficult part of the Pacific Railroad would be its construction over one of America's wildest mountains, the Sierra Nevada. Theodore Judah did more than dream. With scarcely a thought to the remuneration he might possibly receive, young Judah devoted ten creative years to a study of the practical means of laying a railroad over the Sierra, to selling the scheme to California businessmen, and to lobbying for the approval of Congress. When the Pacific Railroad Bill was finally enacted into law in 1862, Judah wrote his partners: "We have drawn the elephant. Now let us see if we can harness him up."

More than two hundred miles of the route of Judah's Central Pacific Railroad (which ran from Sacramento, California, to Promontory, Utah) was above 6,500 feet altitude. Judah's plans required that a dozen tunnels be chiseled and blasted through the granite cliffs of the Sierra. For that part of the track which was not tunnelled, thirty-nine miles of peaked snowsheds had to be built to protect the road from avalanches of snow.

When the first transcontinental railroad was finally completed on May 10, 1869, the joining-of-the-rails at Promontory was celebrated in all the principal cities of the nation. Unfortunately, Theodore Judah did not live to see this monument to national unity completed. A victim of the Yellow Fever, he had made his contribution in the form of preliminary surveys, engineering blueprints, and the prodding of a lethargic public to get on with the task.

The remarkable story of Theodore Judah is told admirably in the chapters that follow. An authentic American hero, this young engineer is brought to life in Helen Hinckley's fascinating biography. Miss Hinckley's careful research and talent for writing have been happily combined to give us an authoritative and readable life of an inspiring and creative young American.

LEONARD J. ARRINGTON

January 1969

Table of Contents

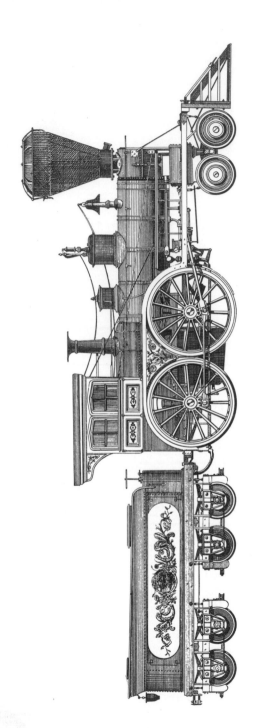

The locomotive *Sacramento* of the Sacramento Valley Road. – SOUTHERN PACIFIC COLLECTION

ONE

Theodore Dehone Judah

"I HAVE JUST the man to work it out for you," Governor Horatio Seymour told Charles Lincoln Wilson, who had come from California to New York looking for an engineer to build the first railroad on the Pacific Coast. "He has just put a railroad through Niagara Gorge that is a marvel of engineering. His obsession is the Pacific Railway. His name is Theodore Judah."

To back up the Governor's statement of confidence in the twenty-seven year old engineer was Judah's impressive railroad record. At thirteen Judah had completed the Classic Course at Rensselaer Institute in Troy, New York, and had taken up transit and chain to work under the famous civil engineer A. W. Hall on the Schenectady & Troy. It had taken only five years to become a surveyor with the full responsibility of an engineer. At eighteen he had gone to work on a road that was to run from Springfield, Massachusetts, to Battleboro, Vermont. From there he had moved to an engineering position with New Haven, Hartford & Springfield Railroad. At twenty he had become the assistant to the chief engineer for the Connecticut Valley Railroad.

The New York State Legislature and the Erie Canal Railroad backers were urging a seemingly impossible project, a rail con-

Anna's eyes were gray-green and there was a definite red glint in her light brown hair. Her feet and hands were small and delicately boned. Most of her life she was a "little on the chubby side" so the waistline in this view must have been achieved with some help from the "stays."
— PIERCE FAMILY COLLECTION

10

nection down the Niagara Gorge. They wanted a road that would connect the ship piers on Lake Erie with Ontario. At twenty-one, Judah had become associate engineer for this road, with the practical planning and construction under his direction. When that work was completed he became chief engineer for the Buffalo, New York & Erie Railroad.

Judah had been married just before he began the Niagara Gorge project and his wife would have been an asset to any young man. Anna Pierce was beautiful, gracious, well educated, gifted in languages and in drawing and painting, and besides she was the daughter of a wealthy man and a granddaughter of Samuel Pierce famed for his fine pewter. In addition to her qualifications and connections there was another plus factor. Anna really loved Judah, had loved him since at the age of eighteen she had met him when he was working in Greenfield where the road from Springfield to Battleboro was trajecting iron over the Deerfield River.

It wouldn't damage Judah's value to the company and to California, Governor Seymour suggested, that he was a Republican, a staunch Episcopalian, and his sympathies were with the North in the rapidly developing national tension. Would Judah's being just twenty-seven be a handicap? No, indeed; California was a land of young men. Four-fifths of the men in San Francisco were under forty. To be forty was to be considered old.

Colonel Wilson was impressed with the Seymours' description of Theodore Judah and asked Horatio to send a telegram. Silas Seymour had been a consulting engineer for the Erie's push over the Catskill Mountains to Buffalo and he knew from his own contact with Judah that the young engineer had a grasp of all of the problems that would arise in building in and over mountains. What none of them knew was that Theodore Judah was already dreaming of pushing over mountains — the Sierra Nevada — and thinking of a project far more extensive and daring than the Sacramento Valley Railroad.

Governor Seymour sent the urgent wire requesting that Judah come to New York City for "an interview of importance."

The four men, Horatio and Silas Seymour, C. L. Wilson and Theodore Judah lunched together in a New York hotel, but it

11

was just two men, Wilson and Judah, who closeted themselves in a hotel room and talked for hours.

Colonel Wilson, massive, affable and very shrewd, had been a farm boy in Maine when he had decided that he wanted to move in a bigger world. He had gone to New York City and somehow made a fortune in transportation. He had left his business to join up for the Mexican War and had quickly gone from enlisted man to colonel. With the discovery of gold in California he had become an argonaut, arriving in San Francisco in December of '49. He quickly became a leading citizen of San Francisco. His first venture — because he knew from his own experience that wealth for him lay in transportation — was a trading steamer on the Sacramento. His schooner served the villages along the river, breaking precedent by steaming above the confluence of the Feather River. He sold out of goods each trip and prices were high. Money was pouring in. Next he built a plank road from San Francisco's North Beach to Mission Dolores which cost him $100,000 and brought in more than $50,000 in tolls the first years. A toll bridge over a slough at Eighth and Mission was his next venture, which quickly paid for itself many times over.

He was now a wealthy man and he married a very wealthy woman, Sarah Jane Rood. They looked about for the best transportation project in which to invest their combined fortune of half a million dollars. What better than a railroad!

Railroad plans had been made and discarded, companies had been organized and collapsed; but Wilson's would be different. C. L. Wilson had never put his hand to anything that had failed. He saw the interminable wagon trains carrying men and freight from Sacramento to the gold country over pitted, dusty, sometimes almost impassable roads toward Negro Bar or Marysville. He would build a railroad that would connect both of these with Sacramento.

A convenient company was at hand. In 1852 a group of farsighted men had figured that men and supplies could come up the Sacramento River to Sacramento City by boat and there take to trains that would run on steel rails following the foothills north to Marysville. Stage and wagon stations could be located along the way and feed into the railroad. As soon as

12

the first stretch was completed and making money to pay for itself, the road could be established eastward to Coloma, where James Marshall had begun the gold rush; northward to Chico, the base of Bidwell's operation; and across the river to Shasta, where Major Pierson B. Reading had discovered gold on Clear Creek and the Trinity. At Shasta the road could communicate by stage with the dozen or more mining centers that had sprung up; towns like Whiskeytown, Horsetown, French Gulch, and Buzzard's Roost. Later, the long river voyage could be eliminated by building a railroad to San Francisco via Stockton.

The backers subscribed $5,000 of what was to be a million dollar corporation. When the company engineer estimated that it would take two million dollars to build the first stretch, the company collapsed. Wilson planned to reorganize the abandoned company. He would not make the mistake of starting out too small. He contacted another wealthy man interested in transportation, Commodore Cornelius K. Garrison.

Garrison had been sent West by the Vanderbilts to bolster their Nicaragua Steamship Line. He had made a small fortune on his own in Panama and California and had become mayor of San Francisco — a position he occupied with sagacity and strength — and put some of his own money into a railroad survey for a line that would unite San Francisco with San Jose.

The Sacramento Valley Railroad was organized August 4, 1852. On August 16, 1852, a board of directors was elected and Colonel Wilson became president. It was October 1853, before articles of incorporation were filed. In high excitement Colonel Wilson left for New York City, the railroad center of the United States. Wilson was a worker, not just a dreamer, but when he dreamed he saw extensions of the Sacramento Valley Railroad organized to go through Negro Bar to Marysville extending to Sonora, Tehama, Shasta, and west to San Francisco — a web of steel rails covering the whole of California.

In the middle of March, 1854, before he met by appointment with the Seymour brothers, the plan had been to contact Robinson, Seymour and Company about materials and to employ W. B. Foster, then chief engineer for the State of Pennsylvania, to be the new road's engineer. Foster wasn't available so Wilson asked Governor Seymour and his brother Silas for recommen-

Theodore Judah spent the first twelve years of his life in an Episcopalian manse in times when churchmen were usually poorly paid. At thirteen he was on his own as a surveyor. Perhaps it was this simple, hardworking background that made him unusually interested in clothes. He wore velvet vests with buttons that might have become collectors items. — PIERCE FAMILY COLLECTION

dations. They agreed that no one could fill the post as well as Theodore Judah.

The long conversation in the hotel room was satisfactory to both men. Wilson was impressed with Judah as a man and as an engineer. Judah was eager to seize the opportunity the Sacramento Valley Railroad presented. Later Judah wrote that Colonel Wilson had told him that each year $50,000,000 in gold was coming out of the sand and gravel from Reading's Bar on the Trinity to Mormon Bar, a short distance from Sacramento; and the entire economy depended upon slow river boats, carriages, stagecoaches, and mule teams.

Judah, his face glowing with eagerness and his mind teeming with plans, sent this message by wire to Anna.

"Be home tonight. We sail for California April Second. Love, Ted."

Early woodcut of Sacramento circa 1849. – SOUTHERN PACIFIC COLLECTION

16

TWO

California's First Railroad

B
E HOME TONIGHT. We sale for California April Second. Love, Ted."

Railroads were building in every direction in New York, Massachusetts, Vermont, and southward, too. Judah was already recognized as one of the finest railroad engineers in the entire country. Why should he want to give up everything he had earned with his ingenuity, his ambition, his energy and his genius to go to California? Years later Anna was to write: "You can imagine my consternation. . . ."

For Judah wasn't asking his wife if she would be willing to change the entire pattern of her life. He was telling her. Evidently he had already booked passage since he gave the date of sailing. And April Second was less than three weeks away.

When Judah arrived home he was aglow with excitement. "Anna, I am going to California to be the pioneer railroad engineer of the Pacific Coast. It is my opportunity, although I have so much here." And later, "Anna, it isn't just this short strip of road for which I shall be chief engineer. Some day the continental railway will be built and I am going to have something to do with it."

They would go by Cornelius Van Derbilt's (Vanderbilt's) new route. His passengers sailed in new vessels to Virgin Bay in Nicaragua. There they disembarked and travelled on a fine macadam-surfaced road from Virgin Bay over the Cordilleras. On the Pacific side they embarked on fast packets that plied the West Coast. This new route was at least two days shorter than the Isthmus of Panama route; it was more pleasant; the ships were new and clean and the rates were lower.

The voyage would take five to six weeks if there were no hurricanes, floods, avalanches of mud or rock to cover the macadam road; no monsoons, no tropical fevers. Judah tried to comfort his wife by saying, "Thousands of people are already in California. If they got there safely so shall we."

Anna answered, "You have made up your mind, Ted. That is all I need to know."

Anna's young brothers, Charles and John, came to New York City to say good-bye to their sister. California seemed as far away as China and they doubted that they would ever see her again.

There were several hundred passengers on the ship. Many of them, like the Judahs, were headed for California for the first time. Many were experienced forty-niners who had brought back fortunes from the gold fields hoping to live happily ever after. They had found that compared with the excitement of the gold fields, life was dull in the sober towns of New England; even in the busy river towns of New York State. They were going back to where fortunes could be made, lost, and made again all in one season.

From the time that Judah had entered Rensselaer Institute he had usually been the youngest in the group. Now he was among men of his own age. Even those who spoke knowingly of Mormon Island, Whiskey Bar, Jimtown, were men in their twenties or early thirties. There was excitement and vitality in the group and Judah found this contagious. He introduced himself as "the engineer engaged to build California's first railroad." Soon everyone on the ship knew him and he spread out his maps while an eager group hung over them, searching out the familiar names and dreaming out loud of the gold still to be had in stream beds and river bars.

They reached Nicaragua without incident, crossed on the fine macadam road without discomfort, and caught the fast packet north to San Francisco.

Now Judah could scarcely contain his excitement. He spent more and more time in railroad conversation and in studying his maps and less and less in sleeping or in walking the decks. As they neared San Francisco he retired to his stateroom where he studied his topographical maps uninterrupted. He showed his wife how much like New York Harbor the Bay of San Francisco seemed to be. The Sacramento and San Joaquin rivers flowed into San Francisco Bay as the Hudson and East River flowed into New York Harbor. But San Francisco Bay was enormous — about 50 miles long and in some places 10 miles wide. "The best natural harbor in the world," Judah said. He pointed out that any railroad that reached the city of San Francisco, a city built upon the tip of the arm of land that embraced the bay from the west, would have to enter from the south with an extra 50 miles of road. He pointed to Sacramento on the map, 75 miles as the bird flies, from San Francisco. "It will take 12 hours by river boat to reach Sacramento," Judah told Anna, "but some day the railroad. . . ."

When the ship docked in San Francisco Bay the sky was a sharp blue; the sunshine was so bright that dancing on the clean water of the bay it almost dazzled the eyes. But once the Judahs were out of the shelter of the ship, the cold wind, so unexpected in the blue and gold of the day, almost took their breath away. Anna found her hair turning to ends in spite of the bonnet tied securely under her chin. The knee length skirts of the frock coats worn by the delegation of men that met them were whipped about the men's legs as they waited on the pier.

"Colonel Wilson, my wife," Judah said as the delegation came toward them. Then Colonel Wilson introduced Mr. Morse and Mr. Carrol, directors of the Sacramento Valley Railroad. There were stockholders with the directors and Judah was delighted to find that most of the men were from New York State or from New England. Some had lived in Troy, others had been astonished at the wonders of the Niagara Gorge Railway or had seen other railroads that he had helped to engineer.

Although at the time the Judahs arrived in Sacramento the city was coarse and new, on J Street where Judah established his railroad office there was constant activity. —

The group moved from the pier to a special luncheon. Judah could scarcely wait for the amenities to be over before he began to discuss the railroad.

He had formulated a plan for discovering how much business the railroad could expect. He asked the directors to place half a dozen careful men at his disposal. These men would be placed at important points along the wagon roads that paralleled the proposed railroad. Night and day for a week they would count the stagecoach passengers and estimate the tonnage in the freight wagons. Meantime he, himself, would go over the route with his surveying instruments and would shortly be able to make a fair estimate of the cost for each mile of road.

"And when do you propose to begin the work?" they asked.

"Tomorrow," he replied promptly.

Two days later, after a brief visit with Judah's brother, Charles, who had reported by slow mail that life in California was just as exciting, rough and raw, just as promising as the rumors and the newspapers said it was, the Judahs began the long day's journey to Sacramento. Anna stood on deck watching the quiet river banks slip by; Judah discussed railroad with the directors who were returning to Sacramento by the same river boat.

In Sacramento Judah became Theodore Dehone Judah, man of importance. He set up his railroad office on the second floor of the Hastings Building on the Southwest corner of Second and J. Street. Anna was installed in rented rooms. From her second story window she could see most of Sacramento. San Francisco had seemed coarse and new, but Sacramento was almost a camp town. Just three years before, a fire had swept through the business district. It was rumored that Collis P. Huntington, the hardware merchant, had lost in building and merchandise more than $50,000. But Hopkins and Miller, next door to Huntington, had lost $55,000.

Now new buildings without charm or grace had been thrown up to take the place of those destroyed. One way the muddy streets were numbered; the other way they were given the letters of the alphabet. The river was the center of the town; from early morning far into the night there were people going and coming toward and away from the river docks and almost

21

always river boats waited at the wharves to be unloaded. There were no buildings higher than two stories, there was little paint, there were no ivy covered schools and churches.

In less than two weeks, an incredibly short time, Judah had completed the preliminary survey and on May 30 he presented it to the directors.

He said that he found the line to Mormon Island more favorable than any other way he had ever surveyed, with no deep cuts, no high embankments, and with a grade so gradual that it was like a slightly inclined plane.

"The route," Judah wrote, "runs from Sacramento, the initial point at crossing of J Street and the city limits, until the location of the yards and station shall be selected, along the north side of the American River to a crossing at Negro Bar, 22 miles . . . . There are no grades of more than ten feet to the mile and these ascending uniformly eastward. In the first nineteen miles there are no excavations or embankments over twelve feet, and for one-half the distance the average is not over three feet and the balance, with two or three exceptions, not more than 5 feet, this taken in connection with easy curvatures and but few culverts or mechanical structures, establish some general facts usually regarded as important elements of success in the future prosperity of any Rail Road enterprise.

They are briefly these:

1st Ability to run trains with rapidity.
2nd Capacity to carry heavy loads.
3rd Present economy in cost and time of construction.
4th Ultimate economy in the cost of operating and maintainance, facts which bear with peculiar weight upon the future operations of your road."

Since there were no engineering obstacles, the final location would depend upon how readily the right-of-way could be procured. The report to the "President and Directors of the Sacramento Valley Railroad" made it clear who would need to be contacted regarding the right-of-way.

"The present line has been run," he reported, "having in view to obtain the shortest distance without regard to the situations of the farms lying on the river, and have therefore been carried in long easy stretches from bend to bend of the river. Should the cost of right-of-way be found too great, a line, perhaps equally favorable as to cost of constructions, may be had by keeping further away from the river so as to avoid the fronts of most of the farms, without materially increasing its length."

The survey was started at the city limits.

"The location into the city not being determined, this survey was commenced at the intersection of M Street with the present city limits, from which point the line runs in a prolongation of M Street, or nearly due east for about three miles, nearly parallel with, and distant southerly from the plank road about 1200 feet, crossing lands of Moffat, Keifer, Widow Harper, Collins, McWilliams, Colby, Moore and Hawkins."

(Later Widow Harper would face grading teams with a shotgun.)

No doubt the directors of the Sacramento Valley Railroad had no difficulty in visualizing the route, particularly when they came to such phrases as "Passing about 800 feet south of Berry's house," "Passing south of Whiteside's house about 700 feet," "north of stand at old race course at Brighton about 800 feet," "South of Bowles' house about 1100 feet, and Rooney's about 800 feet."

Judah was careful to consider expense and ease of construction.

"It was in contemplation to cross the river at Mississippi Bar, but recent examinations show this to be next to impracticable, involving unnecessarily heavy expense. I have therefore extended the lines on to the head of Negro Bar, distant about three miles beyond Alder Springs, there finding a most excellent place for crossing, the river narrowing up from half a mile in width with low shores to from 200 to 400 feet in width with bold high rock banks on either side. The line will cross the river here about 80 feet above the water, requiring a bridge of about 350 feet in length, foundations will be in solid rock, at this point we strike into granite which first showes [sic] itself in inexhaustible quantities, it is easily quarried, cuts well, and is of excellent quality, a specimen of it can be seen in the granite front of Adam's [sic] and Co. new building at Sacramento."

The pencil men stationed at the city limits and J Street and at Lisle's bridge counted stages, stage passengers, wagons, wagon passengers, riders on horseback, foot passengers, mules, cattle. The only moving things excluded from the count were peddlers and drivers. Judah announced that from this tally it was determined that the traffic, both passenger and freight, to and from the gold mines was heavier than anyone had suspected. He was especially interested in the transportation of heavy equipment.

In the early days of the gold rush all a man needed to make a fortune was a shovel and a pan, and perhaps a mule to carry these meager supplies. But now, in 1854, much of the gold available to the lone prospector had been removed. There was still gold, plenty of it, but now it must be washed out of banks with heavy pressure jets of water or mined from the rocks by traditional deep rock mining. Both of these methods required heavy equipment that was difficult to carry in wagons. Judah was most optimistic, "With such a road and such a business it is difficult to conceive of a more profitable venture."

He also had studied costs. He found that common labor could be procured for 50 cents a day, skilled labor at $50 a month. The material which had to come around the Horn would be the greatest expense. The freight cost he estimated at $25 a ton.

He estimated the material which would be needed — locomotives, cars, bridges, buildings, culverts, turntables, rails, ties, and "all things necessary." He had built enough railroads in the East to know the cost of such things. His preliminary estimate was $33,000 for each workable mile of road including rolling stock — an estimate that he was soon to revise upward.

"This will yield the owners of the Sacramento Valley Railroad a dividend of 7½% per month." In conclusion he said, "It is worthy of remark that you have in your hands an enterprise which for merit, and as a means of profitable investment, is unrivalled by any road ever constructed. Its cost is light, its grades are remarkably favorable, it can be built in a few months, its profits will be large and certain."

Even while he was making these surveys and formulating his report he had time to talk to the eager young men who climbed the steps to the railroad office in the Hastings Building; he had time to make friends with the young editor of the *Sacramento Union*, then the greatest newspaper on the West Coast. Editor Lauren Upson reported every step of the railroad operation in his paper.

With the preliminary report accepted, Judah settled down to work. By June 20th he and his surveyors had reached Alder Creek, 18 miles from Sacramento.

Often on a weekend Judah with his surveying equipment and Anna with her sketching supplies loaded on a mule left his surveying camp together. They spent the time picnicking in the foothills, hiking up the gulleys, sketching, taking endless measurements. Judah's work was inaccurate; he was taking altitude measurement with a barometer and atmospheric pressure could be changed by the weather, but later he expected to verify these readings with other instruments. Always Anna listened to his talk of the railroads. He was visualizing the Sacramento Valley Railroad as the first few miles of a continental system. He pushed an accurate, verified survey beyond Mormon Bar to Folsom's Ranch (Negro Bar).

Judah had promised in his preliminary report that the road could be built in a few months, but it was late summer before he had completed his final estimates and it was November 24, 1854, before a contract was signed with Robinson, Seymour & Company of New York to furnish the rails, the rolling stock, all the other materials needed, including those for way stations and round houses. The cost would be $1,800,000; $45,000 for each mile. Judah had adjusted his original estimate upward to $43,500 for each mile and the actual cost agreed closely with this final figure.

The Seymour in this firm was Silas, the brother of New York's Governor, Horatio Seymour. The Robinson was Lester L. Robinson who, with his brother John, was leaving New York to take charge of the actual railroad construction.

It was not until February 12, 1855, that the preliminary work was completed and 100 men were set to working with pick and shovel. By the beginning of March there were 500 men working on the road.

On the fourth of March Judah took the day off. It was his twenty-ninth birthday. He visited with his friend, Editor Up-

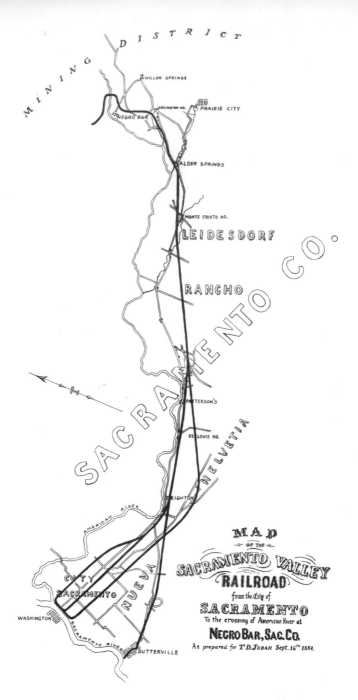

Map of the Sacramento Valley Railroad as prepared
by T. D. Judah, September 16, 1854. — SOUTHERN
PACIFIC COLLECTION

26

son, at the *Union* office and showed him a handsome gold ring. Upson reported the visit for his newspaper.

> On yesterday was exhibited to us by Mr. Judah a handsome ring, manufactured from gold found in the direct line of the railroad now in construction between this city and Negro Bar.

The inscription inside the ring read: "Sacramento Valley Railroad, March 4, 1855. First gold ever taken from earth in making a railroad bank."

On March 28, 1855 the *Union* reported:

> Mr. Robinson, the senior member of the firm who has contracted to complete forty miles of the road, arrived on the last mail steamer and brought with him the bills of lading for the locomotives, cars and most of the iron to finish the road to Negro Bar from this city."

And the *San Francisco Journal* of April 16, 1855 declared that

> The bills of lading show that freight alone on the materials now enroute via Cape Horn for the Sacramento Valley Railroad amounts to $12,000.

The real celebration occurred in June when the freighter *Winged Racer* brought the first rails and rolling stock into San Francisco Bay. On June 15, the schooner *Joseph Hewitt* brought the rails up the river to Sacramento, and the next day the schooner *The Two Brothers* arrived with the locomotive.

Crowds gathered at the wharf to watch the 15 ton locomotive *The Sacramento* and 400 tons of rail unloaded. A great shout went up as the locomotive was lifted by winches and eased onto the wharf. There were many in the crowd who had openly declared that the railroad was all talk. Now the locomotive that had been 130 days in the sailing vessel rounding the Horn was actually in California. This was a new day. A new Era.

Although the grading wasn't completed, Judah began the laying of rails on August the ninth and supervised the assembling of a handcar. He wanted to keep the enthusiasm for the railroad bubbling. Two days later he, Morse, Carroll and Lester Robinson all bent their backs together and lifted the handcar onto the rails in a sort of devout ceremony. All four climbed aboard and rode for a hundred yards. They were the first men to ever ride on a Pacific Coast railroad.

But now, with everything seeming to go so well, the railroad met with money problems. There had been a dry winter which had led to a gold panic and Sacramento Valley Railroad stock began to be forfeited for nonpayment of assessments. Banks failed and C. L. Wilson, president of the company, had his funds in one of these banks. Affable, shrewd Colonel Wilson, who had never put his hand to anything that failed, was in deep trouble.

The *Alta California* for July 30, carried this appeal:

> Grading and bridges are complete almost to Negro Bar. Rails are here now, and fifty cars and three locomotives are on their way. We may soon expect to hear the Iron Horse snorting up and down the Sacramento Valley, leaving the ox wagon and the muleteer only as things of memory . . . . Freight from San Francisco to the mines is enormous. Several heavy laden steamers, besides sailboats, are leaving daily. Freight from Sacramento to the mines is using 700 teams. It seems that this is a field for capital such as exists nowhere else in the world.

The Sacramento Valley Railroad Company was forced to modify its contract with Robinson, Seymour & Company. Instead of going through to Marysville for the present at least, the road would end at Negro Bar. Just above the bar Judah had surveyed a town to be called Folsom that would, temporarily, be the end of the line.

On the evening of August 10, the directors met at Musicians Hall on Eighth Street. They named a new president of the company, Commodore Garrison. William Tecumseh Sherman, head of the banking house of Lucas & Turner, a bank which had not gone under in the panic, was named vice-president.

But the men on the streets knew little of the financial difficulties of the road. Judah kept them railroad conscious with the help of the friendly editor of the *Sacramento Union*. Lester Robinson, too, saw the value of public relations. Shortly after the four had poled themselves a few hundred feet on a handcar, a few pieces of rolling stock were coupled to the *Sacramento* and 200 people were invited to take a ride behind a steam locomotive.

Upson wrote:

> We availed ourselves yesterday of an invitation extended by

the contractors, Robinson, Seymour and Co. to participate in a short excursion behind a locomotive to 17th and R Streets, the present terminus of the Sacramento Valley Railroad. The train, consisting of three platform cars, was densely crowded, as was also the tender, with about two hundred of persons, representative of all classes of our citizens, and started from the levee half past six o'clock, amidst the cheers of the excursionists. The transit was made smoothly and pleasantly to the manifold pleasure of the participants who cheered occasionally as the train proceeded, especially when passing knots of outsiders who were sprinkled along the route as spectators. On the stoppage of the train at 17th Street, some small wags among the guests respectfully requested the engineer to "go on," "take a turn down K Street," "get over on the plank road," and etc. Order having been restored finally, honorable M. S. Latham was called upon, and briefly addressed the assembled crowd . . . The excursion having been made on the first trip of the pioneer locomotive on the pioneer railroad in California was exceedingly interesting and marked an epoch in the history of the city and of the state, although the distance was short, and the incident was unattended with imposing ceremonies. Another trip will be taken on Monday next, which will be participated in by representatives of the press and other invited guests from San Francisco.

The excursion for "Monday next" came off as planned. Judah himself worked the throttle. A *San Francisco Alta* journalist wrote: "Away we sped quite merrily, being forcibly reminded of the times when the scream of steam whistles were hourly heard and a trip in the cars was a luxury that might be enjoyed daily."

At the end of the two mile ride 16 of the guests transferred to carriages to follow the route to Negro Bar. The dusty carriage journey was somewhat of an endurance test. The guests praised the bear steak dinner at Meredith's hotel in Negro Bar; they praised the railroads and their future, but no one offered to invest money.

On October 18 the Robinsons attached all the railroad's property on their contract and a few days later the courts placed the Sacramento Valley Railroad under a deed of trust and appointed J. Mora Moss as trustee.

Judah, who had known all about railroad engineering was

SACRAMENTO VALLEY RAILROAD, TRIAL TRIP OF AUGUST 17, 1855.
From an illustration in the *Pictorial Union*, Sacramento, January 1, 1856.

A festive group climbed aboard the Sacramento Valley Railroad cars for the first trial run and onlookers, almost as jovial, lined the route. From a woodcut illustration in the *Pictorial Union*, Sacramento, January 1, 1856. – SOUTHERN PACIFIC COLLECTION

Sacramento Valley Railroad depot on Front Street, along the levee at Sacramento. Conveniently located across the street was the shop of Adams McNeill & Co., wholesale grocers and agents for the California Powder Works. —

now learning about railroad financing. He pushed himself harder than before.

At the foot of R Street John Robinson and his workmen were building passenger and freight cars. The wheels and the necessary iron work came around the Horn from Boston. Under Judah's direction the rails were extending at a rapid rate. On November 10th the railroad earned its first money. A military company was transported to Patterson, nine miles out of Sacramento, and back. The round trip cost the military $50.00. On the 27th the road was completed to Alder Creek and another excursion party rode to the end of the track. Now everyone knew that the railroad was a reality. After this initial excursion any one who had a dollar could ride to the end of the line. Grown men waited with their restless children to have a turn on the remarkable thing. "We want our children to have a ride on this thing," they said, still unwilling to admit what rid-

THE PASSENGER TRAINS

Will leave the Depot at the foot of K Street, Sacramento, at 6 1-2 A. M., 1 P. M., and 4 P. M. [Sundays excepted.]
Folsom for Sacramento at 7 1-4 A. M., 12 M. and 5 P. M. [Sundays excepted.]
Auburn Station for Sacramento at 6 and 10 1-2 A. M.   Lincoln for Sacramento at 6 and 10 3-4 A. M.

ON SUNDAYS, Will leave Sacramento at 6 1-2 A. M.
Will leave Folsom at 12 M.

Places to and from which Stages run in connection with the Cars:

Stages run to connect with Cars either at Lincoln or Auburn Station.

Sac. and Nevada Line.
Foster's Ranch Cottage,
Globe Ranch,
Wolf Creek,
Boston Ravine,
Grass Valley,
Nevada,
Orleans Flat,
Negro Hill.

Passengers for Orleans Flat and Forest City, lay over at Nevada all night.
Passengers for Downieville, Monte Christo, etc., take Mule Trains to Forest City.
Stages leave San Juan, daily, for Moore's Flat, Red Dog, Marysville, Rough and Ready, Alpha, Omega, White Cloud, Hess' Crossing, Comptonville, and all parts of Middle Yuba.

S. V. R. R. Office, Sacramento,
February 20th, 1863.

Stages connect at Auburn Station.

Sac. and Auburn Line
Forest Hill and Nevada,
Rattlesnake Bar, *Station and Horseshaw Bar,* [*Post Office.*
Whisky Bar,
Franklin House,
Mountaineer House, *Station.*
Auburn, *Post Office.*

Nevada and all connections.

Sac. & Iowa Hill Line.
Junction House,
Yankee Jim's, *Post Office,*
Forest Hill,
Todd's Valley,
California House, *Station.*
Ned-burgh, [*Post Office*
Illinoistown, *Station.*
Cold Springs,
Mountain Springs, *Post Office.*
Dutch Flat, *Station.*
Iowa Hill.

Stages connect at Folsom.

Sac. and Coloma Line
Mormon Island,
Rolling Hills,
Joe Taylor's or Willkashaw's,
Green Springs,
Pleasant Grove,
White Oak Flat,
Somerset House, [*House.*
Cold Springs, *Stop at Somerset*
Uniontown,
Coloma,
Spanish Flat, three miles from Coloma,—*Ticket to Coloma.*
Kelley's and American Flat, two miles from Coloma—*Ticket to Coloma.*

Sac. & Georgetown Line
Salmon Falls,
Centerville,
Maine Bar,
Pilot Hill,
Oak Valley, or Bailey's,
Knickerbocker Ranch.

☞ SEE DIAGRAM OF ROUTES ABOVE. ☜

Murderer's Bar, *Stop at K.* Greenwood Valley. [*Ranch*
Georgetown.

Stages connect at Folsom.

Sac. and Jackson Line
Michigan Bar,
Arkansas Diggings,
Forest Home,
Willow Springs,
Drytown,
Amador,
Sutter,
Fiddletown,
Volcano,
Jackson,
Mokelumne Hill,
Butte City.

Stages connect at Folsom.

SACRAMENTO,
Placerville and Overland.

WASHOE LINE.
Mormon Tavern,
Clarksville, or Spanish Tavern

Duroc Ranch,
Prairie House,
Buckeye Flat,
El Dorado Ranch,
Shingle Springs,
Mud Springs,
Diamond Springs,
Placerville, or Hangtown,
Lake Bigler,
Van Sickles,
Genoa,
Carson City,
Dayton,
Silver City,
Gold Hill,
Virginia,
Aurora,
Esmeralda,

WASHOE.

☞ Logtown and Newtown Passengers Ticketed to Mud Springs, and Grizzly Flat Passengers to Diamond Springs.

J. P. ROBINSON, Superintendent.

The 6 P. M. Train out from Sacramento, connects with the Stages for all of the above named Places, and Passengers procuring Tickets at the Ticket Office of the Railroad, under the What Cheer House, will be sent through the same day.
The Stages run from the above named Places, to connect with the 12 M. Train from Folsom, arriving in Sacramento one hour before the San Francisco Boat leaves.

Wall poster timetable of the Sacramento Valley Railroad dated
February 20, 1863, showing map of rail and stage lines in the
Central California region. — SOUTHERN PACIFIC COLLECTION

ing the cars meant to them. To many this first few miles meant a promise that sometime they could go back home — just for a visit, maybe — without taking the hazardous trip across the plains, the long trip across Nicaragua or the Isthmus or the still longer voyage around the Horn.

Judah ran excursions whenever possible and business was brisk on the partly completed road. The men were working day and night to complete the road to the new city of Folsom. There were now four locomotives on the line The *Nevada* had arrived from Boston, the *L. L. Robinson* from New Jersey, and the *C. K. Garrison*, earlier called The *Elephant* because of its size, from San Francisco where it had been used to level sand dunes.

By Christmas time plans for a gala celebration at Folsom were complete. Judah was disappointed that the company couldn't push on to Marysville as it had originally planned, but he had confidence that the second step would come in time. As far as the road to Folsom went he was proud of it. It was strong and good and would certainly be a suitable first fragment of a transcontinental road.

The locomotive *L. L. Robinson* of the Sacramento Valley Road. T. D. Judah is standing beside the engine tender. – SOUTHERN PACIFIC COLLECTION

33

Sacramento Valley's locomotive No. 4 *Pioneer* was built in 1849 by the Globe Locomotive Works of Boston and shipped around Cape Horn to San Francisco where it arrived in 1854. Originally called the *Elephant,* changed to *C. K. Garrison* in 1855, and to the *Pioneer* in 1869. Was named *Pioneer* because it was the first locomotive to arrive in California. (BELOW) Depot, roundhouse and machine shops of the railroad at Folsom. — BOTH SOUTHERN PACIFIC COLLECTION

At Folsom there were already railroad shops, a roundhouse and a sandstone depot. Because stage and freight lines would converge there, there were also stables and barns. The Meredith Hotel was being extended and new shops and houses were in every stage of construction. The celebration would take place on Washington's birthday, 1856.

The trip to and from Folsom was to be free, so early in the morning most of Sacramento waited to board the cars. There was the powerful *Sacramento* with six passenger cars — strange cars with flat roofs, tiny high windows and uncushioned seats — and a string of platform cars behind it. A group of people who had come up from San Francisco, twelve hours by boat, piled onto the last platform cars not knowing that only the first two were attached. At eleven the *Sacramento* pulled out. There was a wail from the people loaded onto the stationary platform cars. Shortly the *Nevada* appeared and was coupled to the remaining cars.

For a time the *Nevada* kept in sight of the smoke from the Sacramento but abruptly the speed slackened and finally the last car stopped dead on the track. Everybody poured off the cars and up to the engine. John Robinson was in the cab with the engine crew, all three kneeling before the open fire door. A flue had burned through, water was pouring onto the fire and the *Nevada* was out of service until it could be repaired.

John Robinson was the hero of this occasion. He sprinted two miles to the stage station, procured a horse and galloped off to Folsom. The rest of the company had followed to the stage station at a slower rate and there "partook of refreshments liquorish in character". After a time the *Sacramento* came whistling back and, coupled to the flat cars, took the rest of the party into Folsom hours late for the planned program.

But still there was oratory. Senator Flint, standing on a chair on the station platform, told the crowd they were witnessing the inauguration of a railway that would "span the continent and embrace the two oceans." This was Judah's sentiment exactly. There were other speakers, too; Commodore Garrison, William Tecumseh Sherman, Lester Robinson. Even C. L. Wilson, who was now only a member of the board of directors, was called on to "say a few words."

Lithograph of the Sacramento waterfront (1856-1860) showing wharf boat and a landing stage which allowed for the changing level of the river. On the neat expanse of Front Street, drays, wagons and a Sacramento Valley Railroad train at the right, complete the scene.—JOHN H. KEMBLE COLLECTION

The *Sacramento* was going back to the city for the crowd who intended to come for the evening ball and whistled for the excursionists who wished to go home after seeing the town of Folsom and enjoying the excursion. No one wanted to go. The cars went back to Sacramento almost empty. But they returned again heavily loaded. Dressed in high style and low style, the Californians celebrated what no one doubted was the first lap of a continental railroad. The line to Folsom cut a full day from the long haul from the city that was the center of supplies to the mines where the supplies were needed.

Now when the train roared into Folsom, 21 stages were lined up on the crowded, dusty streets to take passengers to the mountain villages, to the mines, or later over the mountains to Nevada's Washoe country. In the town passengers had time to patronize the shops that advertized "Home made pies and cakes," "Novels to rent," "Home cooked meals." Some travellers returning to their homes in the East by stagecoach had shortened their journey by taking the train to Folsom as if one day saved were important. What had once been J. L. Folsom's ranch above Negro Bar was now a metropolis.

To the average citizen the railroad seemed to be taking in drifts of money. In the month of October 1856, the freight trains carried 38,327 tons of freight and the passenger cars were always overcrowded. The cost of the road had been a little less than $60,000 a mile; almost twice as much as Theodore Judah had at first estimated.

But the directors of the road were worried. Already the mines that were reached by the fanning stage lines were less remunerative than those newly opened in Nevada. Some towns and villages had completely disappeared. Wells Fargo, always an enemy of the railroad, had cut its wagon rates and threatened to boycott hauls out of Folsom. More important, the company still owed $700,000 to Robinson, Seymour & Company. The railroad earnings were being devoured by interest payments on the indebtedness. Under the trusteeship J. Mora Moss the company was paying 30 per cent on its floating debt and 10 per cent on its bonds.

The strip of slender rails from Sacramento to Folsom was all the company could complete, though C. L. Wilson still dreamed

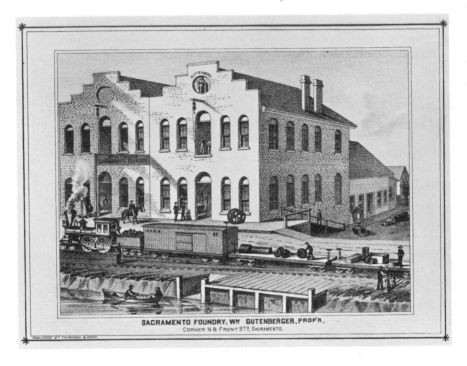

SACRAMENTO FOUNDRY, WM. GUTENBERGER, PROP'R.
CORNER N & FRONT STS, SACRAMENTO.

The Sacramento foundry operated by William Gutenberger, was served by the Sacramento Valley Railroad. The lithograph appeared in Thompson and West *History of Sacramento County.*
— HUNTINGTON LIBRARY, SAN MARINO, CALIFORNIA

of extensions. The projected road that would some day, the planners had hoped, go as far north as Shasta would not be completed in that decade nor the next.

Theodore Judah, still the chief engineer of the Sacramento Valley Railroad, now had little but the high sounding title. There was no work to be done.

Anna didn't ask, "Theodore, when do we go home?" She knew her husband better than that. Too often she had heard Judah talk to others of the need for the railroad that would commence in California and drive up and over the Sierra Nevada. Too often on their weekend picnics in the mountains and foothills she had listened to him talk about elevation, rise, geological structure. She had watched him work on profiles of the area. "Anna," he would say, "some day the railroad will run down one of these ridges. But which one? I am the man who will decide this."

Sacramento was now the capital of the state instead of the Mexican capital of Monterey. The San Joaquin Valley was one of the richest ranch countries in the world but already the farmer was pushing back the rancher and planting fruit and gardens. Judah and many others knew that there were deposits of coal and copper to be mined and marble and soapstone and granite to be quarried. Miles of primeval forest offered fir and redwood for the cutting. And all of these resources waited for the railroad.

A Sacramento Valley train rolls past the picturesque farm of James Cornell at Brighton, just fourteen miles northeast of Sacramento. The lithograph appeared in Thompson and West *History of Sacramento County.* — HUNT-INGTON LIBRARY, SAN MARINO, CALIFORNIA

THREE

Judah's *Practical Plan for Building the Transcontinental Railroad*

E VEN BEFORE THE Sacramento Valley Road had opened for business, Judah was working on an extension of his railroad dream. Each time that he had travelled from San Francisco to the city of Sacramento by slow river boat he had been impatient. Twelve hours! With a railroad, cutting off all the loops and bends that the river made in its meandering course to the sea, and with trains travelling faster than any boat, hours could be cut from that time. Even before his arrival in San Francisco, when he had spread out his maps in the public rooms of the vessel for the interested to study, he had pointed out the looping course of the Sacramento and had predicted that a railroad would soon join Sacramento City and San Francisco Bay.

Now that his energy was no longer needed on the Sacramento Valley Road he determined to do something about shortening the distance between the Bay and California's capital city. There wasn't any strong group of supporters already incorporated to push such a road; no C. L. Wilson to borrow the money and finance the original survey.

Theodore Judah decided to become a promoter himself.

Nothing in his experience had prepared him for the role. He

knew how to engineer a road from the first reconnaissance through the surveys to the actual placing of track; he was prepared to estimate the costs of labor and materials. He had means of making an educated guess regarding the need for the road and the value of lumber that might be acquired with the right-of-way. But he had always been a paid employee and he had no training or experience in promoting, financing, organizing. Armed only with his own boundless enthusiasm, his unquenchable optimism, he began the promotion of a railroad from the city of Sacramento to the Bay. This, he thought hopefully, could connect with the already completed short line and become the first section of a road that would sometime span the continent.

His black eyes flashing, his face flushed with excitement, he described again and again to anyone who would listen the value of the proposed road. And he did get backing for a complete survey. He started the survey in the village of Washington, directly across the river from Sacramento, carried it west to Putah Creek, then to Davis Ranch, over the Montezuma Hills, past the village of Cordelia to Benicia. For a short time Benicia had been the seat of the California legislature. In 1856 it seemed to many — especially to the backers of the Judah survey — that it would be a·major city.

Theodore attacked the survey with his natural whirlwind enthusiasm and energy. He made an estimate of the need for the road by placing watchers on parallel wagon roads to count the coach travellers and guess at the tonnage carried over these roads. He studied the loads of the river boats that plied the Sacramento. He completed a careful survey of route and costs. In February he made a report of his survey just at the time that final arrangements were being made for the celebration of the completion of the Sacramento Valley Railroad at Folsom. It was not Theodore Judah's way to look back at a completed job. He was forever looking forward to the next challenge, as his report of the Sacramento-Benicia Survey shows:

"There is still another light in which your Road may be viewed, which adds additional importance to, and argues still more favorably for this enterprise. It is its connection with the great Pacific Railroad. This subject has been a fruitful source of discussion and has for a long time engaged the attention of many distinguished individuals, both here and at [*sic*] the East.

"While the partizans of the various localities differ as to the merit of their respective routes, all concur in the great importance and absolute necessity of the early construction of this great work. The limits of this report will not admit of a discussion as to the relative merits of these routes, but if built upon any but the Southern route, your road will be the grand avenue of approach to the metropolis of the Pacific. Viewed in this connection it assumes an importance which will not fail to commend it to the attention of all clear thinking and sagacious men, and there is no doubt but if proper exertions were made in the right quarter, that the aid of government would be cheerfully extended to facilitate the construction of this, as of all other Railroads in California, tending to hasten the completion of the great Pacific Railroad, by a donation of public lands for the public good." February 1856.

But the survey report didn't engender the enthusiasm for which Judah had hoped. It was not until years later that a road following closely a large part of this survey was built. Judah turned his attention to other surveys.

Some historians believe that Judah also surveyed a line between San Francisco and San Jose during this period, but of this we can't be certain. It is likely, however, since everywhere people were talking and thinking railroads and Judah was the outstanding surveyor and engineer in the entire West.

Then, abruptly, the period of free flowing gold ended. The easy-to-reach gold, that which could be dislodged with a pick or washed from the streams in a pan, had all been taken out. Receipts from placer mines grew smaller and smaller. Whole towns and villages disappeared as completely as if they had never existed at all. Men who had once panned gold on the edges of streams, who had caroused in noisy saloons and slept in hastily built camps and rooming houses, were now on their way to the new mines across the mountains in Nevada. Had the Sacramento Valley Railroad been completed in 1852, the year in which the building company was first incorporated, it would have paid for itself within a year. Now it was just a "feeble strip of iron" running out from Sacramento. Its chief value was to shorten by one day the journey across the mountains to the new gold fields in Nevada.

To many this seemed the end of western railroad activity. To Theodore Judah it was a challenge to push the railroads faster and farther. Although he still had the title of chief engineer of the Sacramento Valley Railroad, he was no longer actually employed. The company could not go ahead with the roads they had projected. Judah sought other paying jobs to meet his expenses.

One of Judah's commissions was to survey a wagon road across the Sierra to the mines in Nevada. He undertook the commission with enthusiasm. This was an opportunity to come to grips with the mighty mountains he had been studying. Where a wagon road can go, thought Judah, there, with some modifications, can go a railroad.

During the summer of 1856 he disappeared into the Sierra for weeks at a time. He wrapped his transit, barometer and gauges in chamois bundles and strapped them to a pack mule's back. These long trips were too arduous for Anna. She watched him go and waited for his return. She was proud of her husband when she heard it said again and again in Sacramento that no one knew the Sierra as Theodore Judah did.

Now Judah was assuming a new role. He had organized private backers for the Sacramento-Benicia Survey, but in his report to them he had spoken of government support. The California State Legislature convened in Sacramento and Judah determined to get aid for the railroad, at least as far as the Nevada border, from the state. Whenever he was in Sacramento, Judah, turned lobbyist, tried to contact the legislators and persuade one or more of them to introduce a bill for providing state aid. He talked to them on the streets, in their offices, in the homes of friends. But his enthusiasm was not enough. Many of them had seen the plight of the backers of the Sacramento Valley Railroad. Others felt that such a road would not serve their constituents who lived far beyond the proposed roads. No state legislator would lend his name to such a bill. Finally Judah gave up in disgust. "Men of no vision," he called them when they could not even see the value of a proper survey to the Nevada line.

In his report to the Sacramento-Benicia backers he had mentioned public lands. Perhaps even then he had decided to try to get assistance from the Federal Government.

"Anna, you are going home for a visit," he told his wife. "I have decided to go to Washington."

Judah was not the first man to think of asking railroad aid from the Federal Government. As early as 1824 — two years before Theodore Judah was born — Congress had authorized the President to cause necessary surveys for canals and roads to be made, and while the railroad was not mentioned in the act, funds and surveyors authorized by it had surveyed the route of the Baltimore & Ohio Railroad. From that time memorials to Congress regarding railroads were frequent and insistent. In 1845 the first proposal for a transcontinental road had been made by Asa Whitney; he had suggested a road from Lake Michigan to the mouth of the Columbia. This memorial was followed in 1846 by one from George Wilkes, another from Robert Mills, another from Hartwell Carver. Carver promised "births [sic] for sleeping, kitchens for cooking, dining halls and parlors." Ebenezer Allen and Dennis Keenan each offered a project for a southern route.

In 1853 William Gwin, a United States Senator from California, had introduced a Bill in the Senate calling for three transcontinental railroads. Senator Gwin, who had come to California from Tennessee just before the first constitutional convention in '49, had deep pro-slavery feelings. He knew that the central route would serve the interests of California best, but his feelings for the South would not let him push the central route in opposition to a road that might sometime effectively unite the South. On March 3, Congress had commissioned Jefferson Davis, then Secretary of War in the Pierce administration, to survey the three routes: Northern, Central and Southern. Money had been appropriated and the survey had been assigned to army engineers. Such legislation could be counted on to block all further activity.

But in 1856 Fremont was running for the office of President of the United States on the Republican ticket with the slogan: *Freedom, Fremont, and the Railroad.*

If Fremont were elected, railroad legislation would most

The quiet frame house on Federal Street in Greenfield, Massachusetts, where Anna grew up. While Theodore Judah was prodding Congress to action on railroad legislation, Anna waited here for his terse letters of disappointment or his exuberant ones of success. — PIERCE FAMILY COLLECTION

certainly be offered in both the House and the Senate, Judah thought, and he knew that he had something very special to contribute to the discussion of railroad problems. He had actually built railroads in the West — at least one railroad — he had experienced the problems of finding private backing for railroad surveys — at least one survey. He had studied the Sierra Nevada, which, with the Rockies, would be the natural obstructions to the continent-spanning railroad of which he dreamed.

Anna packed only a few of their belongings. They would be back in California, her husband said, before she would need an extra pair of gaiters. Besides, she would enjoy shopping in the East. They travelled by way of the Isthmus of Panama instead of by way of Nicaragua. While Judah had been building the Sacramento Valley Road, Aspinwall & Company had built a railroad across the narrow land-neck that separated the Atlantic from the Pacific.

When they arrived on the East Coast Theodore took Anna to her family in Greenfield before he went to Washington and took rooms on 14th Street.

Although Washington was being built on a beautiful and grand plan, in 1856 most of the public buildings were unfinished and stood like raw "Greek temples on wide muddy roads."

Paris, London, Vienna, all of the great capitals of the world were beautiful cities, centers not only for government but of commerce and culture. Washington was nothing but an unfulfilled dream. But Theodore Judah had not taken the European grand tour; nor seen old world cities. He had come directly from Sacramento and San Francisco, so this city, begun on a grandiose plan when San Francisco was sleepy Yerba Buena and Sacramento was still a part of the wilderness, may have seemed impressive to him. Between the pretentious buildings, the Capitol, the Post Office, the Patent Office, the Treasury, the Smithsonian Institution and the White House there were "magnificent distances."

What concerned Judah was not the physical condition of the city, the open sewers, the filth-filled gutters, but the "feel." From the time he arrived in Washington he felt the tension that was growing between the North and the South. The slaves of the Southern legislators loitered on Pennsylvania Avenue in front of such hotels as The National and Brown's. Seeing the slaves reminded Judah that Washington was in reality a Southern town and his New England instincts, his deep moral convictions, made him feel uneasy. His rooms on 14th Street were not far from Willard's, the most important hotel and busiest bar in the city. It was to Willard's he must go in order to talk with legislators who might be induced to think about a transcontinental railroad.

In spite of Senator Gwin's pro-South sympathies, in spite of his having presented the bill providing for the survey of three roads, Judah had put his hopes on the Senator from California. Surely he could see that California's interests would be best served by a railroad that followed the Mormon Trail, Central California route. Senator Gwin was courteous but he refused to support a Northern route against a Southern.

And as Judah talked with more and more congressmen and senators he understood Senator Gwin's position. There was an extremely delicate balance between the North and the South being carefully preserved in both houses of the legislature. To disturb the balance would uncover the hostile feelings of sectionalism that threatened to break Washington and the nation in two. Judah learned that all the important army positions were held by Southerners. Northern officers like Halleck, Hooker and Burnside had resigned their commissions and gone back to private life. He learned that the social life of the capital was dominated by Southern hosts and hostesses and by Southern mores and ideals. He also heard from many legislators, though no one dared test the truth of the statement, that any legislation that set the North and the South against each other would prove that Southern sympathies dominated in this area as well as in the others.

Judah was sharp enough to see the problem, but optimistic enough to feel he could solve it.

This, he decided, was not the time to suggest that the Federal Government build a central railroad either through direct appropriation or land grants, but . . . Congress had already appropriated money for surveying three roads. The survey had been completed and the result was a beautiful brochure, *The*

Pacific Railroad Exploration Report. Why not an additional sum for a "proper" survey of one of the routes? A survey of the Central Route could be made for $200,000. With a proper survey Judah was certain that he could get private capital to build the railroad.

But no one would listen to him. In the public rooms of the National, Brown's, Willard's, and all the lesser hotels the talk was all of the right of States to withdraw from a union that no longer served them. Not one legislator would dare to present a railroad bill even though he, himself, felt that the railroad might be a good thing.

Unable to find listeners who would hear him out, Judah decided to reach the legislators in a different way. He wrote a pamphlet, *Practical Plan for Building the Pacific Railroad.* He signed himself T. D. Judah, Chief Engineer, San Francisco.

In it he wrote that the project for the construction of the Pacific Railroad was "the most magnificent project ever conceived," and said that it had been "in agitation for fifteen years." He traced the progress of the project in this way:

"Our wisest statesmen, most experienced politicians, scientific engineers and shrewdest speculators, have each and all discussed the subject in [sic] nearly every point of view, and given the results of their wisdom and experience to the world.

"Yet —

"Their projects have proved abortive. Their schemes have failed. The world has listened with attentive ears to the words of eloquence and wisdom from the lips of great and wise men.

"Yet —

"This project has not been consummated. The road has not been finished. It has not been begun. Its practicability has not been established. A survey has not been made. It has simply been made the subject of reconnaissance."

With a copy of the *Pacific Railroad Exploration Report* before him, Judah wrote:

"When a Boston capitalist is invited to invest in a railroad project it is not considered sufficient to tell him that somebody has rode [sic] over the ground on horseback and pronounced it practicable. He does not care to be informed that there are 999 different varieties and species of plants and herbs, or that grass is abundant at this point; or Buffalo scarce at that; that the latitude or longitude of various points are calculated to a surprising degree of accuracy, and the temperature of the atmosphere carefully noted for each day of the year.

"His enquiries are somewhat more to the point. He wishes to know the length of your road. He says, let me see your map and profile that I may judge of its alignments and grades. How many cubic yards of the various kinds of excavations and embankment have you, and upon what sections? Have you any tunnels and what are their circumstances? How much masonry and where are your stone? How many bridges, river crossings, culverts and what kind of foundations? How about timber and fuel? Where is the estimate of the cost of your road and let me see its details? What will be the effect on travel and trade? What business and revenue? All this I enquire to know, in order to judge if my investment is likely to prove a profitable one."

He said that the *Exploration Report,* the result of the 1853 legislation, was "vastly interesting and of little use." He didn't blame the army engineers for the uselessness of their report: "If directed to ascertain distances by latitude and longitude, or with a rodometer instead of a goniometer, they do so; or, if directed to ascertain the altitudes with a barometer instead of a leveling instrument, they do so. If ordered to survey 2,000 miles at the rate of 20 miles per day, they obey orders and ask no questions; but it is no less true that the former means give only general and interesting, while the latter give practical and useful results. The one tells us that the route abounds in obstacles and difficulties or is inexpensive and easy of construction; while the latter determines what these obstacles and difficulties are, or how easy and inexpensive the character of the route is."

Judah's "practical plan" called for a survey carefully planned and adequately financed which would furnish definite estimates, profiles, curves, quantities, all the data that would be needed before construction began. He closed this section with a statement that made clear his whole plan of progress. "Who can doubt with all this information, obtained in a practicable manner, everything deduced from actual calculation, and reduced to dollars and cents, that capitalists can be found who will invest in such a project, provided it can be satisfactorily shown that it will be remunerative."

He then discussed the possibility of quickly shortening the distance between the East and the West by building a preliminary wagon road along the surveyed route. He wrote of snow problems, of hostile Indians, of operational costs, of the development of stronger locomotives, of probable rates and tariffs. He also considered the danger of mortgaging America's future by mortgaging the road to European speculators.

He closed the pamphlet:

"And be it remembered that it is not the through lines to California alone upon which the road is to rely for through travel. There is Utah, Oregon, Washington, the Russian possessions, the Sandwich Islands, China and the Far East Indies — all of which are brought, more or less, within the influence of this road.

"It is hoped and believed by many that Congress will, at this session, pass a bill donating alternate sections of land to aid in the construction of either this enterprise, the wagon road, or both. Should this be effected it will obviate the necessity of adhering strictly to the plan as herein proposed; but whether or not this is done, it does not alter the justice of the conclusion as to the proper steps to be taken in making such a survey as is proposed, and locating the wagon road upon it.

"There are numerous points in the proposed plan which will no doubt appear to many as bold, startling and apparently impracticable; but if its boldness will have no other effect than to induce sensible men to read and reflect upon them, the desire of the writer will have been gratified."

It must have been with a feeling of accomplishment that he delivered the manuscript to the printer, Henry Polkinborn; and with a feeling of impatience that he waited for the booklet to reach the legislators.

Who would have guessed that few legislators even took time to read the copies that were delivered to them? They were stacked with other things on overflowing desks, or thrown away to litter the already poorly kept streets of the capital.

Judah had hoped that his carefully planned, carefully worded plea would at least stimulate discussion and open the way for him to talk with men of prominence. It did neither. Even those who scanned it were not interested. The West? What was that? An open underdeveloped country given over to Indians and buffalo without an organized state, scarcely a settlement, except that of the Mormons, between Iowa and California. Nebraska Territory stretched from the Missouri River to Utah; Dakota and Washington from the Pacific to the headwaters of the Mississippi. The men that Judah had hoped to reach understood the rich plantations of the South, the whirring wheels of industry in the North, but the West! California, of course, was something else again, and so was the Nevada Territory with gold so easily come by. But California was easily reached by packet down the Atlantic Coast and up the Pacific. And wasn't there a fine new railroad connecting the two routes by spanning the Isthmus? The rest of the West was as far away as Hong Kong or St. Petersburg.

Gathering up the few undistributed copies of *Practical Plan* Judah left Washington for Greenfield. Here was his audience, here the one person who never tired of hearing about a transcontinental railroad. In Greenfield Anna waited.

To her he poured out his frustration, his anger at those who would not hear. Anna had seldom seen him in such a mood.

Then abruptly his old optimism replaced the despair. If the railroad were a working project the Government would have to see that the Mormon Trail-Central California Route was feasible. That was it. In coming to Washington he had attacked the problem from the wrong end. The transcontinental railroad would have to begin in California.

FOUR

"Crazy Judah" and the Railroad Convention

EFORE JUDAH AND ANNA arrived in San Francisco he had formulated a new plan, a new approach. If the Federal Congress wouldn't listen to the voice of one man, certainly it would heed the voice of an entire state, perhaps of the entire West Coast. He planned to persuade the California State Legislature to call a Railroad Convention which would memorialize Congress in favor of a transcontinental railroad over the Central California-Mormon Trail route.

He had failed once in his attempt to get any legislator in Sacramento to promote a railroad bill. This time he would ask for something else. A convention could bring together important, forward looking men from every area, and their voices would speak for the West. As soon as he landed he would begin the groundwork for the calling of such a convention.

But as soon as he landed there was other work to be done. He was still chief engineer for the Sacramento Valley Railroad and while he had been in Washington some work had accumulated. There was a new project calling him, too.

Judah's old friend, Colonel C. L. Wilson, crowded out of control in the Sacramento Valley Railroad and disappointed that a road projected to run from Sacramento to Marysville had ended

The California Central railroad bridge across the American River at Folsom with a passenger train on its way to Lincoln. The problems of construction mentioned in Judah's report are clearly seen in this photograph taken May 31, 1858, when the bridge was commenced. — SOUTHERN PACIFIC COLLECTION

at Folsom, had determined to do something about his shattered dream. He had taken his plans directly to the people of Marysville. There, in 1857, the California Central Railroad was organized with Wilson as president and T. D. Judah as chief engineer. Wilson hurried East to raise additional capital and Judah, leaving Anna in rented rooms in Sacramento, went directly to the end of the line at Folsom and began the survey. Although his survey showed that trestles would be needed to cross ravines and swamps, at least one large cut through a bluff would be required, and a tremendous bridge over the Ameican River would have to be built — a span 216 feet in length and 92 feet above the river bed, that would cost $100,000 — still Judah's preliminary report was enthusiastic.

The California Central was an interesting challenge and Judah was excited about it. Not only should it help C. L. Wilson, his friend, to recoup some of his losses and make money for other stockholders but it should be a valuable asset to the Sacramento Valley Railroad, practically smothered by its enormous debt.

The work of construction on the new road was begun the last of May 1858, by C. L. Wilson & Company. Seven months later on the last day of December, Judah reported to the president and directors of the company that five miles had been completed — five difficult miles. Judah's report on the work of the first seven months of construction is specially interesting because it shows exactly how Judah worked when he was building a railroad. He began with the heaviest work first, the building of the bridge across the American River. He reported that the bridge was almost finished and that track could be put down in February. He described the difficulties of making cuts through solid rock, decayed granite, and cement gravel and he reported how much of the material moved from the cuts was used in the fills.

When a public road wound around the side of a hill crossing the projected railroad line twice, once on grade, Judah surveyed and built a thousand feet of new public road that obviated any crossing of the rails. He wrote, "Considerable expense has been incurred in making these changes, but it is believed they will prove of permanent value to all parties interested."

He had brought timber from Puget Sound for the trestles be-

SACRAMENTO VALLEY RAILROAD.

SUMMER ARRANGEMENT.

On and after the 15th of March, the Trains of the Sacramento Valley Railroad will leave as follows, viz:

PASSENGER TRAINS WILL LEAVE

Sacramento daily........at 7½, A. M., and 3½, P. M.
Folsom daily ...... at 7¾, A. M., 12 M., and 5, P. M.

On Sunday, besides the above, there will be from Sacramento a 10, A. M., train.

FREIGHT TRAINS WILL LEAVE

Sacramento...............at 7½, A. M., and 2, P. M.
Folsom .... at 7¾, A. M.

☞ The 7½ A. M. train will take through freight only.
☞ No freight transported on Sundays.

STAGES

Connect with the 7½ A. M. trains out for

NEVADA,	GRASS VALLEY,	AUBURN,
IOWA HILL,	FOREST CITY,	DOWNIEVILLE,
ORLEANS FLAT,	OPHIR,	GOLD HILL,
ILLINOISTOWN,	YANKEE JIM'S,	GREENWOOD VALL'Y
GEORGETOWN,	MORMON ISLAND,	COLOMA,
EL DORADO,	DIAMOND SPRINGS,	PLACERVILLE,
PRAIRIE CITY,	MICHIGAN BAR,	COOK'S BAR,
WALL'S DIGGINGS,	LIVE OAK CITY,	ARKANSAS DIGGINGS,
WILLOW SPRINGS,	DRYTOWN,	AMADOR,
SUTTER,	JACKSON,	FIDDLETOWN,

And all the Intermediate Places.

RETURNING—the Stages will connect with the 12 M. train in arriving at Sacramento, in time for the San Francisco boats.

☞ For freight or passage apply at the Railroad Stations.

J. P. ROBINSON, Superintendent.

1857 summer time schedule of the Sacramento Valley Railroad as it appeared in the *State Register*. — SOUTHERN PACIFIC COLLECTION

cause "The conditions of first class Road require that all Timbers used in work of this kind should be durable and of a superior quality; that in planning the same, no pains or expense should be spared, in rendering the *strength* and *safety* (italics Judah's) of the Structure absolutely unquestionable, all other considerations being of minor importance in comparison with that of safety and durability."

He ended his report by saying, "Thus it will be seen, that the heaviest and most difficult part of the work has been taken hold of and prosecuted with a commendable spirit of energy and perseverance which, followed up, will complete your Road to Marysville within twelve months."

The first five miles had cost $500,000 and this in a time of panic, but when Judah built he built forever.

The Buchanan Panic of 1857-1858 was felt from the Atlantic to the West Coast. Gold seekers out of work, were going back to the river bars and gravel banks in the hopes that some gold might have been accidentally missed. Word had got around that the Chinese were making a good thing of this type of gleaning and the little men with the denim pantaloons and the long pigtails were increasingly unpopular with the miners who felt that native Americans should have any gold that was to be salvaged from the worked over gravel. When placer mines had given out quartz mining had begun, and men who had hoped to pick up shining nuggets in the mountain streams were employed at extremely low wages to bring the quartz out of the mountains in the traditional manner.

The principal hope of the new Central California and of the Sacramento Valley Railroad was that the heavy machinery needed for this type of mining and the food and other supplies needed for the miners had to be transported from the Sacramento River to the mines. This was the purpose for which C. L. Wilson and other investors had promoted the road back in '52. But Wells Fargo had always been against the railroad and the lowered freight rates the company offered together with a partial embargo on goods that went part way by train and the attempts of the city of Sacramento to tax material unloaded on its wharfs and reloaded on to the trains all cut into the money the railroads had expected to make. There was another bidder for freight hauling, too. A big effort was being made in Shasta County, at the upper end of the Sacramento Valley, to deepen the river channel so that river schooners could bring materials· all the way from San Francisco Bay without the problem of loading and unloading and changing carriers.

If the railroad was to continue to have its share of freight it would have to fight for it. Judah had always been a fighter. Perhaps he knew that the failure of the Sacramento Valley Railroad would discourage the building of others and make his big dream, a transcontinental span, impossible. Judah, surveyor, engineer, promoter, lobbyist, became a warehouse to warehouse, street-to-street solicitor for railroad business. Always as he solicited business he talked of the convenience, the speed, the dependability of the railroad and the possibility that the railroad would soon be extended past the Sacramento River Valley to cross the Sierra and run eastward.

Often he told Anna that he was astonished at the apathy of the men he talked with. Everyone wanted a railroad, but no one wanted to have a part in building it.

Years later Bancroft, the California historian, wrote:

"The sunburnt immigrant, walking with his wife and little ones beside his gaunt and weary oxen in mid-continent; the sea-traveler pining on ship board, tortured with mal de mer; the homesick bride, whose wedding trip had included a passage of the Isthmus; the merchant whose stock needed replenishing; the miner fortunate enough to return home — everyone except, of course, the Pacific Mail Steamship Company, prayed for a Pacific Railroad. And they did nothing but pray, when it is a well known maxim that the gods wait for a beginning before they lend their aid."

Theodore Judah was determined that he could make that beginning. He was glad when he received an assignment to make a reconnaissance survey of the Sierra Nevada, working north from the South Fork of the American River. Whenever a surveying job was offered he took it and went to work with his usual whirlwind effort.

His trip to Washington had been expensive: transportation both ways for himself and Anna in "decent accommodations," his long stay in the room on 14th Street, the cost of entertaining the men whom he had tried to talk to, and the publication and distribution of *The Practical Plan*. Some historians believe that Anna paid some of these expenses. If she did she never mentioned it in her reminiscenses, travel accounts or letters.

Whenever Judah was in Sacramento he spent all of his time talking to people, on the streets, in the hotel lobbies, on the wharf. Always he talked railroad, and always the men to whom he talked reminded him that these were hard times, Buchanan's Panic. Remember? In such times the dream of spanning the continent with a railroad was a "pipe dream." And it takes "more than one drop of water or one clap of thunder to make a rain storm."

But still he explained to anyone who would listen that it would be perfectly possible for the California State Legislature to call a railroad convention. This wouldn't cost anybody any money. Such a convention could memorialize Congress for assistance in building a Central Pacific Railroad, and such a memorial might break the deadlock between the slave and free states.

The Butterfield Stage Route had just been opened up over the route suggested by President Buchanan. The route went from St. Louis to El Paso, Texas, through the Southwest to Los Angeles and thence up the coast to San Francisco. With the fastest horses only a few days were saved over the steamship route that took passengers over the Isthmus on the Aspinwall railroad or across Nicaragua. The journey was more tiring, far less comfortable and more expensive than by water and the cost was prohibitive for freight. Besides, there was always the danger of hostile Indians.

The opening up of the Butterfield Route, a disappointment to everyone, gave Theodore a new talking point.

People that he could not reach with the sound of his voice could read his arguments in the *Sacramento Union*. Lauren Upson, the editor, was still his friend and his greatest admirer. He wrote: "We have just talked to Theodore Judah about plans for the Pacific Railway. This amiable Engineer believes that . . ." and then followed in the words of Judah (perhaps he had written them himself) the reasons why the Central California-Mormon Trail route was superior to any other route that had been suggested.

It was a good thing that Upson called him "amiable." Other Sacramento men were beginning to describe him with another adjective.

One day Newton Booth, a wholesale grocer in Sacramento, stood on the corner of 7th Street talking to John A. McIntyre. He shoved McIntyre toward the door of a shop, saying, "Here comes crazy Judah."

McIntyre had never seen an insane man and he was curious so he insisted on waiting on the street until Judah passed with a quiet, "Good morning, Mr. Booth."

"Crazy?" McIntyre asked.

"Oh," Booth said, "he is a skillful engineer and he isn't crazy about anything but a railroad across the mountains. But on that subject he is a monomaniac. I have been forced to tell him never to speak to me on that subject again."

Of course Anna heard what was being said about her husband. In her memoirs she wrote: "Everything he did from the time he went to California . . . was for the great Continental Pacific Railway. Time, money, brains, strength, body and soul were absorbed. It was the burden of his thought day and night, largely of his conversation till it used to be said, 'Judah's Pacific Railroad crazy.'" She told him what the people were saying about him and urged him to not try to reach their deaf ears. "Theodore, these people don't care," or perhaps, "Theodore, you are wasting your thunder." He would laugh and say, unperturbed by Anna's concern over his reputation, "Anna, we must keep the ball rolling."

In the evening, Theodore sat in the light of the coal oil lamp and planned his strategy for pushing through a resolution in the legislature. He worded and reworded the resolution that would be offered for acceptance. Although he would never be a legislator he would formulate more railroad legislation than any other man of his time.

Finally, April 5, 1859, the legislature passed the resolution to call a convention. To the convention would be invited not only representatives from all of California but from Oregon, Washington and Nevada as well. As soon as the resolution was actually passed setting the convention date for September, Judah wrapped his instruments in chamois again, strapped them to his pack mule and was off to the mountains. He had not yet found a suitable pass through the mountains, a pass that could make the building of the road possible. If he could only locate it before the convention met!

Then, too, he was interested in a new project — or an extension of one already in progress.

He was chief engineer for the Sacramento Valley Railroad running from Sacramento to Folsom bringing men and materials 22 miles closer to the mines. He had joined C. L. Wilson and some citizens of Marysville in pushing the construction of the California Central from Folsom to Marysville. Lincoln, a new town laid out by Judah was the temporary terminus of the California Central. From Lincoln the rails would run north through Marysville and sometime on to Shasta; but the quickest way to the Nevada mines and the possible first miles of his dreamed of transcontinental railroad would have to be toward the east. Clearly an extension, even a short one running east from Lincoln toward Auburn would be valuable.

The project that Judah was working on in the late summer and early autumn of '59 was not too ambitious but it would be a beginning. The Lincoln-Gold Hill Rail Road, sometimes called the Eastern Extension, would cover only seven miles of the distance.

Lincoln was a new town but Gold Hill seven miles east and a little north on the banks of Auburn Ravine was a thriving mining town with more than 1,000 people.

Judah surveyed the route and ordered the iron for the short line from England. He stated that the expected railroad would be in operation by the time the California Central was completed and that the two roads would share equipment.

Editorial writers in the *Nevada Democrat,* the *Auburn Signal* and *Sacramento Union* protested that the steep grade between Gold Hill and Auburn would make the final link with Auburn impossible. To Judah nothing was impossible.

While Judah was pushing through the final surveys and using every available hour for further reconnaissance in the mountains Anna was in Sacramento. She seldom joined him even for week ends as she had during his earlier reconnaissance trips. She had a great deal of work to do before September. Her

Theodore appreciated Anna's taste in clothing. He particularly enjoyed seeing her in ruffles and bows. — PIERCE FAMILY COL-LECTION

knowledge of the mountains, of the problems associated with railroad building, of costs, of the need for a transcontinental line was second only to her husband's. Now she covered her table, her sofa, even her floor with his notes, clippings about his work, clippings about the failure of the Butterfield line to bring any real transportation improvement to California, profiles he had prepared, statistics he had accumulated. These she sorted and organized. She reduced the information to charts and graphs, and tables that would be self-explanatory and give visual proof of the value of the Central route. From morning until night she bent over the materials. Her combination of a wide background in engineering gained from listening to her husband's talk, her own keen intelligence, and her skill in visual arts made her work a tremendous contribution. When she packed the material to take to San Francisco she put with it her own paintings and sketches of the Sierra.

When Ted returned to Sacramento for an occasional weekend he found Anna thinner and somewhat pale. He urged her to spend her afternoons visiting friends. But this was impossible to the "weaker" half of the Judah Railroad promotion team.

September 20, 1859, the convention opened in San Francisco at the Assembly Hall on the corner of Post and Kearney Streets. There were more than 100 official delegates from every county in California and from Washington and Oregon. The lobbies and bars of adjacent hotels were crowded with the "hangers on," men, women, and even children who were related to the delegates or simply there because this was a place of excitement. John Bidwell was elected president and he had two vice presidents, Edwin Landor of Washington Territory and Alexander P. Aukeny, of Oregon. Judah was the representative from Sacramento but he was careful to not get himself elected to any office. Obviously he had the convention in his hands. He had been the master mind behind the whole thing and some folks even whispered that he was paying the bills. Besides, who else knew so much about railroading?

Anna, dressed in quiet good taste, circulated among the delegates and found that several of them actually represented the Pacific Mail Steamship Company, Wells Fargo, and other freighting companies. They had come to the convention to block its work. To everyone she was gracious and charming, but in her busy mind she was taking a poll — how many would back Judah's proposal—, how many would oppose it?

Most of the delegates had come prepared to support special routes. Those from the north favored Noble Pass — a pass from Shasta City to the big bend of the Humboldt River in Nevada. As early as 1852 the people of Shasta had raised $2,000 to prove the feasibility of this route. William H. Noble had guided a party through the pass travelling 300 miles in eight days. In 1855 the California legislature had memorialized Congress to make this a principal military route and prior to the convention there had been a reconnaissance survey completed. If the Sacramento Valley Railroad were extended to Shasta it could join a road through the Noble Pass. The Noble Pass boosters believed such a road would have the support of all the northern mining and ranching country.

Proponents of other routes came just as well prepared to press the selection of their roads. Judah knew that the entire time of the convention could be spent debating where the terminus should be, what pass the road should take through the mountains, and then dwindle into nothing at the end. He wanted the convention to do just two things:

1. Ask for a Central Pacific Railway survey that could be the basis for construction, leaving all questions of routes to be decided *after* the survey was completed.

2. Suggest to Congress the manner in which the Federal Government could best promote the construction.

He still believed that private capital should build the road but somehow the risk must be taken out of the investment. He had been close enough to the Sacramento Valley Railway to realize that private investors must have some protection before they would be willing to put up millions of dollars. He thought that if the Federal Government would guarantee five percent interest on invested capital, men with money could be persuaded to invest it. The government could raise the necessary funds through sale of public lands. Judah didn't want to see the government in the railroad business — he was opposed to government ownership of what he thought should be private enterprises. The money spent to guarantee the interest on investment would be like other funds spent for internal improvements.

The chairman of the convention appointed a committee of ten to draw up the resolution. Thomas H. Pearne, a delegate from Oregon, offered a resolution that the appointed committee be instructed to set forth the preference of the convention for the Central route, "the feasibility of which has been demonstrated by the maintenance upon it, summer and winter, of stage lines." J. B. Crockett of San Francisco was committee chairman but all of the members knew that Judah was the "expert" and looked to him for guidance. Perhaps Judah had "handpicked" the other nine. Late into the night Judah worked on the wording of the resolution so that there would be no ambiguity, no loopholes.

During the convention all sorts of local business was transacted. Judah, working quietly, shifted the focus to the two questions that he thought were most important. Anna, circulating even more quietly and engaging in what most people thought was fascinating feminine chatter, made a mental tabulation of convention opinion. Theodore had told her that it was important that the matter of route was not brought to the floor of the convention until there was certain to be an overwhelming majority of the delegates who would stand up and be counted for the California-Mormon Trail route. Neither Judah nor anyone else knew the exact route that the road should take through the Sierra Nevada, nor what terminus would be most satisfactory. He was honestly willing to wait on the results of the survey before these decisions were made.

October 11, 1859, the Convention adopted exactly the memorial to Congress that Judah had felt was essential.

In addition to the recommendations regarding the building of the road across the territories, the convention recommended that the terminus of the road should be San Francisco, thence to San Jose, thence to Stockton, thence by the most practicable route to the Sierra. No one had the slightest doubt that Sacramento would be the actual railroad center. The State of California would create a fund of $15,000,000 though it would take a constitutional amendment to the California Constitution to do this, and Oregon would raise $5,000,000. If stockholders were relieved of individual responsibility, this pooled amount should make possible the building of the road to the Nevada border.

The Convention's next order of business was to appoint Theodore Dehone Judah to carry the Memorial to Congress. Judah was in high spirits. For the first time in a long time he felt things were going his way — that the railroad he had talked and dreamed of was at last assured. He smiled when people asked if preparing to leave in just a week's time wasn't a hardship for his wife. "Anna always knows the right gaiters," he said.

They sailed on the S. S. *Sonora* on October 20, 1859.

FIVE

Judah Makes Another Try in Washington

WHEN ANNA and Theodore boarded the S. S. *Sonora* they were still in high spirits. Everything had gone so well; there hadn't been a hitch in Judah's plans from the time he had launched his campaign to get the California legislature to call a Railroad Convention until the present moment. There was just one thing that concerned Judah deeply and he put that steadfastly to the back of his mind. In all of his reconnaissance — and he knew the Sierra Nevada better than any other man — he had yet to find a suitable break in that seemingly impenetrable double wall, a mountain pass through which the railroad might pass. Surely there was such a pass. With government funds to make a complete survey it would certainly be found.

As soon as they boarded the ship Captain Baby came to greet them. Theodore was no longer "Crazy Judah;" he was one of the most important men in California. Before the ship left the Bay the Judahs were introduced to John A. Burch who was going to Washington to represent California in Congress. Both Congressman Burch and the Judahs knew that their being on the same boat was no accident. This, like every other move in the long campaign, Judah had arranged.

67

The S.S. *Sonora*, a Pacific Mail Steamship Company vessel set a speed record of 11 days and 21 hours between Panama and San Francisco in 1854. The Judahs and congressman-elect John Burch travelled in style when they boarded her in 1860. WELLS FARGO BANK HISTORY ROOM – SAN FRANCISCO

The two men immediately became intimate friends. Judah loved to talk about the railroad and Congressman-elect Burch loved to listen. When Judah talked about the great national changes that could be expected to follow the building of the transcontinental line Burch found him "gentle, persuasive and charming."

Later Burch wrote, "No day passed on the voyage to New York that we did not discuss the subject, lay plans for its success and indulge pleasant anticipations of the wonderful benefits certain to follow that success." He was amazed that Judah not only understood every technical feature of route survey, road building and railroad operation but also the involved problems of legislation and finance. Judah laughed at his friend's amazement. He had cut his political teeth lobbying for the railroad in the California State Legislature, sharpened them in his abortive attempt to get a bill before the Federal Congress the year before. Finance he understood because of the serious money problems that had almost wrecked the Sacramento Valley Railroad and had made impossible the carrying out of the company's ambitious plans for extension. For every statement he made, whether in engineering or financing, he had the support of careful figures. It was true that he had greatly underestimated the cost of the line to Folsom from Sacramento, but he had learned from experience. He was optimistic and buoyant as a cork.

Also on the S. S. *Sonora* was Senator Lane of Oregon. Unlike Congressman-elect Burch he was not persuaded to full cooperation by Judah's railroad talk. He listened graciously but he never committed himself. Being more experienced than young Burch, he saw the difficulties that railroad legislation would face. Perhaps he also hoped for the Northern Pacific Railroad that Senator Gwin had proposed in his three railroad approach.

One evening as the Judahs dined with Burch and the talk turned, as usual, to the railroad, Anna asked almost innocently, "Would there be any advantage in establishing a Pacific Railway Exhibit?" She described the exhibit she had prepared for the Convention and Burch thought that such an exhibit would be a fine idea. Anna had noted the interest that the delegates to the convention had shown in the maps and charts and graphs. In the week given her for choosing the right gaiters she had packed her clothing in a day, delayed her shopping to do in the East, and had spent her time in packing and adding to the materials they had shown at the convention: samples of ore, minerals, fossils which Judah had collected as he explored the Sierra Nevada. She also packed her own sketches and paintings. Safe in her luggage were all of the materials needed for a Pacific Railroad Museum.

When their ship docked in New York Anna went at once to her family in Greenfield. Judah took the train to Washington. Anna had been such an enormous help to her husband in the San Francisco Railroad Convention that it was surprising that he didn't take her with him to Washington to set up the museum she, herself, had suggested. Perhaps he was reluctant to take her into a city that might be fired by civil war at any time, perhaps he had to consider expenses, perhaps she was homesick and preferred being with her family, or perhaps Judah, bubbling with optimism, felt he could handle this matter himself.

Anna's young brothers began to think that they had wasted tears when they had hurried to New York to say good-bye to her when she had first left for the far away West. Now she seemed to be commuting between the Pacific and Atlantic Coasts and they saw her more frequently than they did their Connecticut cousins.

Washington! What Judah couldn't do in Washington with the Railroad Convention behind him!

Washington! The train depot was more dreary and depressing than he remembered it. He stowed his baggage into a hack. The same Negro slaves lounging in front of their masters' hotels, the same feel of a sprawling Southern town.

It made a Northerner like Judah sick to see that Washington already belonged to the South. A year before he had felt the grave tensions, sensed a sleeping volcano under the city. What would he find now?

After leaving his things in his rented rooms Judah went directly to Willard's. Here he listened to the boastful talk of young Southern clerks. He saw for the first time seccessionist cockades being worn, and he heard about John Brown.

John Brown, "Old Otowatomie Brown," had followed his four sons to Otowatomie, Kansas, in 1854. Here he had not only participated in, but organized much of the bloody fighting that had finally brought Kansas into the Union as a free state. His tactics had been constant harassment of the Southern emigrants who held slaves. Travelling quickly through familiar country a few bold men, like Brown's own sons, could attack a plantation and be gone before the owner had recovered from his surprise. One of the Brown sons had died in the struggle.

With Kansas free, John Brown turned his attention to graver matters. If harassment had been so successful in Kansas why wouldn't it work in the South? Why couldn't armed slaves, set against their masters, abolish slavery in the South? Procuring the arms would be a problem but John Brown determined to supply them from federal arsenals. His father had been an abolitionist, he had taught his twenty children to be abolitionists, but hating slavery was not enough. The time, he thought, had passed for the use of words.

He rented a farm in Hagerstown, Maryland, where he gathered his sons and a handful of other ardent abolitionists. The farm was near the federal arsenal at Harper's Ferry where he planned to acquire the first arms needed for a slave insurrection in the South. His was a pitiful little army, just 22 men, but he took the arsenal and he took the town, but he couldn't withstand the siege of local officers reinforced with government troops under Robert E. Lee. Twenty-two men: ten were killed, seven wounded and in chains, five escaped. Two of the dead were Brown's boys. Brown, himself, was wounded and in chains.

When Judah arrived in Washington John Brown's trial was in progress. John Brown could do no more damage; but Harper's Ferry was just 55 miles from Washington. What John Brown had planned was armed insurrection! The white people of Washington already distrusted the Negroes, especially the free Negroes, and had made stringent laws to control them. Insurrection might flare any day, they thought. Abolitionists in Washington were calling John Brown a hero and saying that only demonstrations like this could draw attention to the "sins" of the South. Slaveholders felt that he had unloosed a force that might destroy the Union before it had subsided. At the time of the siege the government had rushed its complete military force at the capital to Harper's Ferry — 106 marines — and the raid had been called an "armed insurrection."

When Congress opened nothing interested the lawgivers but John Brown, hero or villain, saint or renegade. In both the Senate and the House men almost came to blows. Rumor had it that a fiery Senator from Ohio brought a brace of horsepistols with him to the Senate and placed them on his desk for everyone to see. There was talk that many legislators were secretly armed and some were even practicing sharp shooting. Judah heard every place he went that the vile Republicans had instigated this lawlessness!

How was he, a Republican and a Northerner, to get anyone to listen to him — to receive the Railroad Convention's Memorial? In any hotel lobby he could hear a discussion of the "impending crisis," of the possibility of a division of the Union, of the probability of civil war. In any bar he could hear that the Northerners would never fight. That the military tradition was entrenched firmly in the South.

And because listening to these discussions could not further his purpose Judah stayed in his room and mapped the strategy which he hoped would bring the Memorial before Congress. When the John Brown case was finally finished, Congress would be ready to get down to work. He outlined and arranged appointments with editors, newspaper correspondents, cabinet members, heads of bureaus, congressmen and senators. None of these were encouraging. He even achieved a conference with faltering President Buchanan. Sitting across the table from the silver-haired, aging President, Theodore must have known that the conference was useless. Buchanan's critics said that he was a broken man who divided his time between weeping and praying. Now with his head cocked toward one shoulder in the usual way, his badly squinting eye closed, he gave Judah his best advice. "Forget the railroad, young man, until we see what is going to happen to the nation."

Often Theodore and John Burch met to discuss the railroad, so important to California and evidently so unimportant to everybody else. Burch had not known how helpless a freshman congressman is. Without prestige, without membership on im-

72

portant committees, a congressman could do so little. This was a bitter discovery for both of them.

Disturbed, but not discouraged, Judah made hurried trips out of Washington. He travelled through the East collecting data on railroads and railroad materials. Everywhere he was a welcome visitor. He gained "some reliable information with regard to the operating of engines on heavy grades" which became highly important in view of solving the question of crossing the Sierra Nevada. "Grades as high as 350 feet per mile can be overcome and operated with safety."

Evenings he spent in writing, in drawing maps, in outlining procedures. His articles found space in newspapers and he, himself, distributed his circulars and maps.

December second, John Brown was hanged. His presence at his execution was so simple, so pure, so grand that even his enemies could not doubt his dedication and sincerity; and two years later Union soldiers would march to battle singing

> John Brown's body lies a mouldering in the grave
> But his soul goes marching on.

After the execution Washington was ready to turn its attention to other things. John A. Logan, a congressman from Southern Illinois who not only headed the House Committee on Contingent Expenses but was violently pro-Northern in his sympathies, gave Judah an audience. Logan was amazed at Judah's knowledge of facts and figures to support every clause in the California Railroad Convention's Memorial to Congress. He could see the value of the Mormon Trail-Central California route binding the North firmly together and holding the West, including California, in the Union. He was also intrigued with the maps and charts and graphs, the ore and minerals and fossils, the profiles and sketches and paintings, that Judah had ready to show him. A Railroad Museum! That was a fascinating idea.

Such an exhibit ought to be convenient for senators and congressmen to drop in to familiarize themselves with the possibilities. It also should be open to the public. He assigned Theodore the former Vice President's room in the Capitol for this display. He also arranged for Judah to be allowed to draw upon

73

all of the government departments for additional maps, surveys, reports, anything that would dramatize the need for the transcontinental railroad.

From the first the museum was a success. Being sociable in Washington was growing more and more difficult. Southerners entertained Southerners; Northerners, Northerners. When the two factions met in large social gatherings they spoke on unimportant, non-political subjects. The museum was something almost non-controversial to talk about. Hundreds of people saw the exhibit: congressmen, other lobbyists, government clerks, Washington citizens. As they filed through the exhibit Judah talked and many learned, from the exhibit and from him, more than they had ever known about either the railroad or the West. He knew how to be persuasive. He was courteous, gentle, never excited, never depressed, always entertaining. He spoke of the railroad as if there were no unsolved problems.

Still in the back of his mind was the thought that he had not yet discovered the really good pass through the impassable mountains.

During the Christmas holidays Theodore hurried to Greenfield to spend a few hours with Anna and her family. If she had hoped to return with him to Washington she was disappointed. From Greenfield, he went to Chicago. It had never been a part of his transcontinental railroad plan to form a company to build the entire span. As he saw it his problem was to move eastward through California, probably through Nevada and possibly through Utah and Wyoming. He hoped to find out in Chicago what plans were being made for pushing west from the Mississippi. In Chicago he interviewed officials of the *Chicago & Rock Island Railroad* and the *Chicago, Burlington & Quincy Railroad*. Surely they must have definite plans for surveys west of St. Joseph and Council Bluffs.

A second Railroad Convention was to convene in Sacramento in February. Judah hurried back to Washington and with Congressman Burch drew up a bill that should be presented to Congress. They embodied in it every suggestion made by the Pacific Railroad Convention of 1859 and sent it to Sacramento for approval of the convention. The bill was then printed and circulated to every member of Congress. Any legislator who would take time to read the circular understood the provisions of the bill:

1. The bill was concerned with the construction of a railroad between the Mississippi River and the eastern boundary of California.

2. The government was to guarantee the payment of five percent interest each year for three years on the bonds of the company.

3. The Company was to issue bonds not to exceed $50,000,-000 to constitute a first lien upon the property, assets, etc., of the Company and the Company was to be entitled to the Government's guarantee only as the work progressed.

4. The road was to be completed in ten years.

5. The railroad was to be granted a strip of land four hundred feet wide together with the right of way. There was also to be a grant of 5,000 acres of lands for depots, watering stations, roundhouses, etc.

6. Every alternate section of public lands for twenty miles upon each side of the road was to be set apart and sold to obtain funds as the money was needed.

7. The remaining sections of land were to be guaranteed to the company constructing the road.

8. The Company was to carry the mails for the United States at a price not to exceed $600 per mile each year.

Theodore Judah sent the bill to Sacramento. The Convention enthusiastically endorsed every clause.

Both Burch and Judah knew that the advantages of the provisions of the suggested bill could be understood only with study. Judah had copies printed and distributed to every member of the House and Senate. With the copy of the bill went a circular which supported with facts and figures each clause of the bill. He also had copies of the bill and the circular printed in New York and circulated among men who were thought to be interested in railroads and who had money to invest in such enterprises.

Each day he was in the Pacific Railroad Museum educating everyone who would look and listen. Few people in the East lacked curiosity about the West, especially about fabulous California, and Judah's "knowledge of the subject was so thorough,"

Citizens of Sacramento waiting for the Pony Express rider with mail from the East. The rider stopped at the elevated hitching rack between the Union Hotel and the Post Office on the right.
— SOUTHERN PACIFIC COLLECTION

according to Burch, "his manner so gentle and insinuating, his conversation on the subject so entertaining that few resisted his appeal."

He was determined to not bring the bill before the House before he was assured of a majority vote. This was the strategy which had worked so well at the convention. When he thought that there was no possibility for failure Congressman Burch, with all the enthusiasm and background of Judah himself, presented it.

It didn't even come up for a vote.

For once the buoyant Judah was completely depressed. He wrote to Anna. He closed the Museum. Why, the failure was incredible! Both he and Congressman Burch had known that the minds of the legislators were on the impending crisis between the North and the South; but they had prepared for the passage of their bill so carefully. It was no comfort when an inadequate compromise bill presented by Gwin in the Senate was also tabled though Senator Gwin had everything that John Burch lacked: experience, prestige, acquantance with the "best" people. (It was said that Senator Gwin spent $75,000 a year of his own money in entertaining and in maintaining his mansion on Nineteenth and I Street.)

Then something happened to bring Judah's hopes bouncing up again. On the fourth of April the Pony Express, travelling the Mormon Trail, thence to Carson City, Nevada, to Lake Tahoe and through the American River Gorge into Placerville, made the overland journey in *ten* days. Ten days, and over the Mormon Trail-Central California Route! What a demonstration of the feasibility of a railroad over this same route. What a dramatization of the possibility of binding the East with the West.

Now was the time to work again in California, Judah decided. The bill was tabled only until the next session, and the railroad company with a carefully surveyed route would stand the best chance of getting government support. There was still a pass through the double barrier of the mountains that must be found.

July 1860, the Judahs embarked for Panama. Theodore's discouragement and depression had been deep but not long lasting. Again he was hopeful, even excited. If Lincoln won the next election and the Republican party held the House majority, surely a bill calling for cash loans and land grants — the bill that he and Burch had drawn so carefully — would pass the House and win the approval of the Senate and the President.

On board ship he wrote a report to the Convention. He gave as his reason for failure the preoccupation of everybody in Washington with the danger to the Union. He also drew up a bill for expenses.

For printing bill and circulars in Washington	$20.00
For printing bill and circulars in New York	$20.00
	$40.00

Anna, looking at the bill, asked, "No charge for transportation, Ted? Why, the cost was at least $2500.00."

Theodore smoothed the hair back from her serious face.

"Anna, the transcontinental railroad will be built, and I will have a part in building it."

"I do not know whether I am married to a man or a railroad," she said. But later she admitted that her "adorable lunatic might someday grow violent."

It was hot aboard ship, really sweltering. Anna felt depressed and frustrated by the failure in Washington. But Judah had already turned his mind away from the disappointment. "With facts and figures they cannot gainsay my honest convictions," he wrote. "But I must be able to say not merely, 'There is a route over the mountains;' but 'Here are the maps, profiles and estimates of such a route.'"

His next necessity was to find that route.

SIX

At Last. A Possible
Route Over the Sierra

T
HE EXPERIENCE in Washington had been the most crushing in Judah's life; and he had often been disappointed. Two years of work had been set aside with a simple motion to table the Railroad Bill for consideration at the next session. And who knew what would have happened in Washington before the next session?

On the ship returning to San Francisco he spent more time in his stateroom, less time in talking the continental span with anyone who would listen. He had turned his mind away from failure with Congress and was looking forward to finding that elusive route through the Sierra Nevada — the route the road must follow if it joined any central line from the East. Government help would come later, he was assured of that, if he could just find the passable route. The stateroom grew hotter and muggier as the ship approached the Isthmus, but still Judah bent over his maps deciding what areas he would explore as soon as he reached California. Anna later wrote, "Oh, how we used to talk it all over and over on the steamer enroute to California in July."

But as soon as he reached California there was accumulated work for him to do in procuring more business for the Sacramento Valley Railroad, supervising the work on the California Central and pushing the grading on the Eastern Extension.

During his absence in Washington Placer County had voted in favor of the extension from Lincoln to Auburn; the grading of the road had been begun from Lincoln to a temporary terminus just south of Gold Hill, called Centralia, and the iron rails, spikes and chairs were due to arrive from England in November.

On the 18th of October he visited Nevada City and recommended that teamsters pick up their loads in Folsom instead of in Sacramento when bound for the Grass Valley-Nevada City area. He even offered free use of the Folsom Bridge and for two days free freight on the Sacramento Valley Railroad. Although the *Nevada Daily Transcript* said that Judah was actually advertizing his short line railroad from Lincoln to Gold Hill, the *Sacramento Union* commented that Judah was doing a good job as the agent of the Sacramento Valley Railroad.

A few days later Judah, himself, wrote a letter published in the *Sacramento Bee*. There was no doubt, he wrote, that the California Central and its extension, the Gold Hill and Lincoln short line would be in operation by the first of January, 1861. The grading to Lincoln was finished and the grading to Centralia almost completed. The iron had arrived in San Francisco and the locomotives were on their way from Philadelphia. (He could not know as he wrote so optimistically that a serious illness would keep C. L. Wilson in the East and postpone the completion of the California Central, nor that rail would never be laid on the Eastern Extension. The iron he had carefully ordered from England, all 550 tons of it, would fall into the hands of the builders of the Sacramento, Placer & Nevada Rail Road and be used to build a direct line from Folsom to Auburn. The 550 tons of rails, spikes and chairs were just enough to lay tracks to the granite quarries at Wildwood and complete a quick paying line.) With a burst of energy he put his work behind him in three weeks and was ready to begin his new explorations.

Often he had travelled as far as possible by coach or stage and then had gone forward on foot with a mule to carry his equipment. This time he outfitted himself for independent travel. He purchased a sure-footed steady horse, a light one-seated carry-all. In the back of the carry-all he stored food, camping equipment and his instruments: an anaroid barometer, a compass and an odometer. When the going was too rough for the little buggy the horse could act as a pack animal. It was a fine idea, but it eliminated Anna. She wrote, "The engineer is in the mountains. I am in San Francisco and Sacramento among friends."

At the Railroad Convention the proponents of Noble Pass had supported their nomination with excellent facts and figures. Perhaps Judah would have to find his railroad route somewhere near the headwaters of the Sacramento. But for the present he was determined to find a more central route. Since 1840 immigrant trains had been coming through these very mountains. Certainly one of these passes would be appropriate or at least possible for railroad building.

Without telling Anna where he was going he started for the mountains. Jogging along behind his strong little horse Judah drove into Eldorado County. Directly east of Auburn and north of Placerville like the third point on a triangle, was Georgetown. Here he left his carry-all and started on foot through the mountains. This, he discovered, was not the route for which he was searching. Next, he made a careful mile by mile exploration of Hennessy Pass, leaving his equipage in Nevada City. This was not the route.

Tired and impatient he returned to Sacramento to resupply his wagon. Anna had been trying to reach him with a communication from Daniel Strong of Dutch Flat. Dutch Flat was a mining community in steep hilly country about fifty-five miles east of Sacramento.

As he read, a new life came into his eyes. "I will take the stagecoach at once," he told Anna as he passed her Daniel Strong's communication. For Doctor Strong thought that he had found what Theodore Judah was looking for.

Without delay Judah took the stage to Dutch Flat. Daniel Strong, who had a little drug store in the center of the community, came out to meet the stage. "Theodore Judah," the stage driver said, somewhat awed by the notoriety of his passenger. "And this here is Dr. Daniel Strong."

The two men shook hands and sized each other up. Judah,

At Dutch Flat, Judah and "Doc" Strong began their recon-
naissance of the route that would be followed by the Central
Pacific Railroad. — HUNTINGTON LIBRARY, SAN MARINO, CALIFOR-
NIA

burned from the Sierra sun, bore little resemblance to the suave, embroidered-waistcoated Judah of the Central Pacific Railroad Museum. Dr. Strong was not handsome, but clean and sinewy and strong. Judah liked his firm handshake and thought he looked more like a prospector than a doctor. Judah had a special gift for relating himself to others and in Daniel Strong he found exactly the man to share his enthusiasm. In fact Daniel Strong had a bursting enthusiasm of his own.

While Judah ate a quick meal Daniel Strong talked. He had come to this country in the fifties. By training he was a pharmacist and so he had opened a little shop in Dutch Flat. There wasn't any other doctor in the area and since he knew the use of the drugs he sold and understood most of the common ailments, he had become the town's doctor. His patients' name for him, "Doctor," was a loving rather than an official title; a name Judah adopted, too.

"Doctor" had never been bound by his little shop. He had wanted to stretch out and help to subdue this wonderful country. His dream had been to bring the wagon trade through Dutch Flat to increase the prosperity of the village, so he had set out to find a suitable place to take a wagon road through the mountains. The summer of '59 he had spent most of his time in the mountains with his surveying instruments. Yes, he was a surveyor, too, he admitted with a laugh. Wasn't everyone these days? He had used up all of his money and in June of '60 he had raised money for a survey of the route he had found. He wasn't a real engineer himself, and couldn't make an actual survey, and folks had contributed money ranging from one dollar to ten dollars to pay for a survey. He had wanted a real engineer to do it and when he heard that Theodore Judah was interested in such a route he had sent him the letter. He showed Judah the document dated June 26, 1860, with the names of the contributors signed on it.

Judah spoke not of his abortive attempts to get help from Congress, but of the problems he had met in the mountains since his return from Washington and on his earlier explorations. In all of his explorations he had found the Sierra Nevada not only precipitous, harsh and uncompromising — this he had expected from the first — but they had a peculiarity that baffled him. The Sierra was really two impenetrable walls with a trough between them. Sometimes the trough was 35 to 50 miles wide; sometimes narrow enough to seem an ordinary chasm. But once you got through the first range of mountains there was always the second.

"Wait until you see what I have found," Doctor said quietly.

What Judah had been looking for was a river passage cutting through the mountains. What Doctor Strong showed him was a ridge between two deep river valleys, the south fork of the Yuba and Bear Rivers and the north fork of the American River. This ridge was a long, gradual, almost continuous incline like an elevated pathway from the Sacramento Plain to Donner Summit, 7,000 feet above sea level.

As they pushed on, riding and hiking by turns, Judah grew more and more excited. They were following the almost obliterated trail down which the remnants of the Donner Party had struggled 13 years before. Of course there were many breaks in the ridge, it wasn't any wide, finished road or even a basis for one, but Judah pointed out in his eager confident way that trestles could cross these breaks. Trestles would add to the expense but weren't at all impossible. Where higher cliffs blocked the progress along the ridge, tunnels could be used. Oh, it was an excellent route. Daniel Strong had had a brilliant, creative vision.

The two men hiked on, their horses carrying their equipment and supplies, breaking path as they went and taking readings with their instruments. Judah had not felt so happy since the successful completion of the Railroad Convention. No, that was wrong. Judah had never felt so happy.

At last the two men reached Donner Summit. They looked down upon the brilliant, gem-like blue of Donner Lake cradled in a forest of deepest green. To the south of them peaks rose 2,000 feet higher, snow-crowned and imponderable. From where they stood they could see the Truckee River which flowed north from Lake Tahoe turning east not far beyond Donner Lake. Doubtless it cut a gateway through the second row of mountains. There seemed to be a not too steep descent through a mass of mountains to the Truckee Meadows in Nevada and beyond that was open desert.

When, from the Summit, Judah and Strong saw Donner Lake and the river flowing eastward from it cutting through the second range of mountains, they were jubilant. This was the route through the impenetrable Sierra Nevada range. — GOLDEN WEST COLLECTION

Theodore Judah and Doctor Strong turned and embraced each other. Here, someday, would go a railroad. Judah had many eager questions to ask but Doctor Strong only shook his head. Beyond this he had not surveyed. And so the two pushed on, Judah working in his high speed, methodical manner. Doctor Strong was the best assistant he had ever had on an actual survey.

The two paid no attention to the passing of days, or weeks, or seasons, they were so engrossed in their work, so ecstatic over their progress. One night Doctor Strong, with his special sense of the forests, was awakened by a strange stillness. It was never noisy in the forests but he had become accustomed to hearing night sounds as he slept. He looked out of the tent. Snow was falling softly, silently, but heavily. What's more it had been snowing for some time. He awakened Judah. All of their fine dreams would come to nothing if they were snowed in without adequate supplies. Since no one knew where they were they would perish without anyone ever discovering their plight.

Together, in the dark and cold, they broke camp. Searching for an already obliterated trail in total darkness, they pushed their way through the snowy canyon. When they at last found the trail with the help of their horses they slogged on through the night. Judah's mind was still so filled with the promise of the new route that it was not until later, when he heard Doctor Strong tell of being caught in the mountains in an early snowstorm, that he realized they had barely escaped alive.

Warm blankets, a bed and a few hours sleep in Dutch Flat and both men were ready to work again. Sitting at a table in the little drug store Judah told his friend, "Give me some writing material." Doctor Strong recognized the light in Judah's eyes and brought paper, pen and ink. There was not room on the table so Doctor cleared a part of the counter on which Judah could sort out his notes. From his notes he worked out the first profile of the route of the Central Pacific Railroad.

Doctor went about his business, listening to local news, checking his shelves, tying up small parcels of calomel or asafoetida, recommending mustard plaster for one patient, hot foot baths for another. To those who enquired about the route that the two men had surveyed on the money raised in June, he answered, "It is better than you think."

At last Judah pushed back the papers and laid down the pen. "Doctor," he said, "I shall make my survey over the Donner Pass, the Dutch Flat Route, above all others."

Both men knew that it would be necessary to confirm this initial survey with a much more careful one. They faced the fact that such a survey would cost $500 or more and neither of them had that much in his pocket. Doctor Strong had been away from his drug store more days than he had been in it since he had dreamed up the idea of the wagon road. Theodore had impoverished himself, and perhaps Anna, with the trips to Washington. But if the route meant something to Daniel Strong it meant something to everybody else who would profit by bringing wagon trains through the town. Everybody in town liked and trusted Doctor Strong, and most of the men had heard of Theodore Judah. Together he and Judah canvassed the town and asked everyone who was solvent and would like a railroad through their town to subscribe. One woman contributed two hundred and fifty dollars. Many more contributed as little as one dollar.

From the first, Theodore Judah seemed to consider the Dutch Flat Route the discovery of Daniel Strong although later it was called Judah Pass. When he hurried back to Sacramento, more triumphant than he had ever been, he went at once to see his friend at the *Sacramento Union*. This article was worth headlines in any Western paper.

The article was published November 9, 1860, just three days after Abraham Lincoln, "the black Republican," was elected to the office of President of a rapidly dissolving Union. At the same time that the article appeared in the paper a brochure on which Judah had been working feverishly since the 'find", was mailed. The brochure, entitled *Central Pacific Railroad to California,* said: "Confident of the existence of a practical route across the Sierra Nevada nearer and more direct than the proposed line via Madeline Pass and the headwaters of the Sacramento, I have devoted the past few months to an exploration of several routes and passes through Central California, resulting in the discovery of a practicable route from the city of Sacramento upon the divide between Bear River and the north fork of the American River; which gives nearly a direct line to Washoe, with maximum grades of 100 feet per mile." It also said that the Donner Pass Route was 150 miles shorter than the Nevada-Sacramento Route used by the Army for the 1853-54 *Surveys and Explorations.*

One of those who read the newspaper article and the brochure was L. L. Robinson. L. L. Robinson and his brother John were members of the firm Robinson, Seymour & Company who had contracted the materials for the Sacramento Valley Railroad, who had come West to see that it was properly built, and who had taken over the railroad when the company could not fulfill its contract. Lester Robinson, with Morse and Carrol and Judah, had bent his back and helped to lift the handcar on to the first rails in California and had helped to pole the car a few hundred feet. The third locomotive had been named the *L. L. Robinson.* He was the real head of the company for which Judah worked as chief engineer. When he read the article he was furious. Judah, he said, was an employee of his company, his chief engineer. He claimed that finding this route was part of an earlier survey for a wagon road for which the company had paid. Any discovery of a new route should have been reported to him and the other directors of the company, not to the public. Without calling Judah in to explain his actions, the company dismissed Judah. The dismissal was actually ordered by J. Mora Moss, court appointed trustee of the company, and was executed through John Robinson, but Judah felt that L. L. Robinson was to blame; and he was indignant.

"The Find," Judah said, was not his, but Doctor Daniel Strong's and the mountain people who had raised the money to pay for the long reconnaissance trip that Strong and Judah had completed. Evidently L. L. Robinson misunderstood Judah's statement concerning the "find" belonging to Daniel Strong. Much later he testified under oath that Judah had told him in confidence that he had never made a survey of the Donner Pass Route at all. Actually, Judah had crossed and recrossed the mountains twenty-three times on foot, on horseback, or with his litttle wagon. He had pushed the reconnaissance beyond Donner Lake, determining the best route to follow to the Nevada line and the beautifully flat desert beyond.

Judah and L. L. Robinson, both with railroad dreams, had long been associated. The discovery of the new route, whether reported first to the trustees of the Sacramento Valley Railroad or to the public, would have been invaluable to the Sacramento Valley line that already ran as far as Folsom and might have been the first lap of the projected railroad. But L. L. Robinson was not the man to retract and Judah was not the man to offer an explanation twice.

Actually, having been dismissed was a boon to Theodore since from that time on he could exert all of his energies toward building a railroad to the Nevada line.

The Railroad Bill would come before Congress in December. The bill provided for assistance to a railroad to be constructed under its provision, but also, according to the bill, the California construction must be effected by a California corporation. Theodore Judah was determined to form that corporation and have it named in the bill.

Once again in the drug store of Doctor Strong he called for writing material and drew up what he called "The Articles of Association of the Central Pacific Railroad of California." But it took more than articles of incorporation to organize a railroad in 1860. In the fifties there had been too many railroads on paper, too few that were actually even surveyed, let alone built. The California law required that capital stock in the amount of $1,000 with a ten percent cash payment for each mile of road must be subscribed before the company could be incorporated. Since the distance between Sacramento and the Nevada line was estimated at 115 miles, subscriptions of $115,000 with a cash payment of $11,500 must be made. Judah pushed the paper across the counter to Daniel Strong. "Doctor, sign for what you want."

Both of the men signed for more than they could afford.

It was a big day in Dutch Flat. Nobody minded his own business. Doctor and this fellow from Sacramento were going to put a railroad right through Dutch Flat. Many of the men and women had shown their confidence in Daniel Strong before with contributions large and small. Now everybody dug into his savings. What if he didn't get back East quite as soon as he had expected to? What if he didn't have money enough to send for his girl before the year was out? A railroad would make crossing the continent a summer breeze compared to overland travel or the long voyage by way of the Isthmus.

Riding horseback, the two men visited Auburn, Illinoistown, Grass Valley and Nevada City. Their enthusiasm was so contagious that men in these towns hurried to put down their pledges. Five towns, three days, $46,500 pledged and all bonafide subscribers. This was a great deal of money but still it was less than half enough. $70,000 more was needed. But if this much could be raised in these little mountain towns what could be done in San Francisco now that the ball was actually rolling!

Picking Anna up in Sacramento, Theodore went at once to San Francisco. Anna had scarcely seen him during the summer and fall. Now he talked incessantly not only about the details of the route's discovery and reconnaissance but of what he hoped to do about financing. No one would profit more from the railroad he intended to build than the financiers of the Bay City.

They took rooms in the Russ House. From morning until evening he was gone. Evenings Anna joined him and his associates for dinner but there was no time for anything but railroad talk. After less than a week in San Francisco Judah wrote Doctor Strong: "I have struck a lucky streak and shall fill up the list without further trouble. I have got the richest concerns in California in to it."

Anna was worried about Judah's health. He was giving himself no time to rest, no time to relax. But he was happy. His black eyes were shining with eagerness. The concern and depression that she had seen on his face when he spoke of his failures in Washington had now disappeared. "Theodore couldn't have been happier," she later wrote.

Then came *the* evening. This evening the San Francisco financiers were to add their names to the list of investors started in Dutch Flat. Theodore left Anna at the Russ House. Tomorrow, he thought, the incorporation of the company to build what he had begun to call "my little road" would be possible.

From the time that Judah entered the conference room he must have felt a change in the atmosphere, a difference in the spirit of the men who were already seated at the table. "We believe in you," each said in his own particular way. Then each went on to explain that his present large financial interests would make it impossible for him to extend himself further. Judah couldn't believe that these men who had encouraged him so much had now decided against subscribing toward the railroad. One of them said, "If Congress does not pass a Pacific Railroad Bill no road can be built. If a bill is passed the road can not be completed for ten or twenty years."

Judah answered, "Seven years will build a road under the provision of such a bill as I believe can and will be passed."

"But if the bill isn't passed? If Congress refuses to grant lands and funds for the road across to California?"

"We would still have the road to Washoe," Judah insisted. "I will undertake to build a railroad over this route in two years for $70,000 a mile. A road from Sacramento to Washoe." Then he reminded them of the Comstock Lode in Nevada, of the gold that might pour out to the West Coast over such a line. Of the men and supplies that might pour in. Even if the entire continental span were slow in building, this road would be an excellent investment.

They pointed out that there was a provision in the California State Constitution that stockholders were liable for their proportion of all debts and liabilities of any company in which they had stock. Suppose the transcontinental line were never built or wasn't built until 20 years had passed. Many of the richest gold strikes in California had already played out. When would that happen to the Comstock Lode? In such troubled times. . . .

Judah felt in the room the same tensions that he had known in Washington. He remembered President Buchanan, pathetic in indecision, with his side-tilted head, his nearly closed eye, his face filled with weariness: "Forget the railroad, young man, until we see what's going to happen to the Union." Lincoln was a different man from Buchanan, a man who would see the railroad as essential to a united country.

Wearily the men heard Judah out, but they were adamant.

He returned to Anna, shaking with anger.

"Anna, if you want to see your friends in the morning you must pack your bag and trot around to see them, for I am going up to Sacramento on the boat tomorrow afternoon. Anna, remember what I say to you tonight, so you can tell me sometime; not two years will go over the heads of these gentlemen I have left tonight, but they would give all they hope to have from their present enterprises to have what they put away tonight. I shall never talk or labor any more with them. I am going to Sacramento to see what I can do with the citizens and loyal businessmen of that city."

SEVEN

Four Storekeepers
of Sacramento

O NCE MORE "Crazy Judah" walked the streets of Sacramento. Anna, worried about how thin he was growing, how tired his relaxed face looked as he slept,
wished that her husband hadn't undertaken "the work of
giants." It seemed to her that nobody appreciated Theodore except, perhaps, a handful of friends. She knew that acquaintances
on the street were telling each other that Judah had never
been a really sane man.

Judah brushed off her concern. He had written to Doctor
Strong about his disappointment with the San Francisco financiers and had promised to keep him informed about progress
in Sacramento. Doctor Strong had agreed to take the stage
down to Sacramento whenever anything "looked promising."
Judah still had excellent relations with the *Sacramento Union*
and he had a close friend in James Bailey, a jeweler, the only
really wealthy man that he knew personally. Bailey had promised to "come in" when other investors could be interested.
Judah had also talked with the Robinson brothers. Relations
weren't friendly between them since Judah had been dismissed
from the Sacramento Valley Railroad employ, but the Robinsons were railroad men, and they owned a stretch of track from

Sacramento to Folsom which might very well become a part of the new road.

Finally, when he felt he had aroused enough interest, he held a meeting at the St. Charles Hotel on K Street. There were present mostly old friends and acquaintances: A. P. Catlin, his attorney; Charles Marsh of Nevada City; B. F. Fleet, the young surveyor; the Robinson brothers and a few others. To them he described his reconnaissance over the mountains; he explained the route that Doctor Daniel Strong had discovered in looking for a wagon road and of which he, himself, had made a preliminary survey. He talked about finances, too, and the possibility of Federal aid if the bill, tabled at the last session of Congress, were passed at the next. He explained what State aid from California and Oregon could do to help finance the project. All that needed to be done now was to subscribe $10,000 a mile for the proposed route. Already more than a third of the necessary amount had been subscribed by forward looking men from five mountain towns.

But there was no gleam of interest in the men who sat in the St. Charles Hotel. These men were much less interested than the San Francisco financers.

As the men filed out one stopped to say, "You are going about this thing in the wrong way. If you want to come into my office some evening I will talk to you about the road."

Judah's despair fell from him like a discarded coat. The man who had made this promise was Collis P. Huntington, and Collis P. Huntington was the shrewdest business man in Sacramento. He had often discussed a possible railroad with men who frequented his hardware store. He had contributed to building a wagon road from Placerville to Carson City. He had helped to build the telegraph line. He knew the mountains and their difficulties. Now he had invited Judah to discuss his "little railroad." After all, the meeting had been a success.

The next day Judah met Charles Crocker, another important storekeeper in Sacramento, on the street. As usual he began to talk about the railroad and mentioned Collis P. Huntington as a man who might be interested. Judah and Crocker might have known each other years before in Troy since they were both boys there at the same time. But Charles Crocker, nicknamed

Bull at that time, had been selling newspapers at the Hudson Ferry and the Rensselaer-Saratoga Terminal, keeping other boys off his beat with blows and curses when Theodore had been attending classes, visiting railroad operations, and listening to seminars at Rensselaer Institute. Now, Crocker, his big, practical hands folded together behind him, listened to Judah's talk; then said slowly, "Well, I'll watch which way the cat will jump."

That evening Judah climbed the stairs to the office above Huntington's hardware store at 54 K Street. Huntington invited Judah to talk about the project and said almost nothing himself. When Judah finished he invited him to come the next night to his brother-in-law's home on K Street between 9th and 10th Street. Some "interested men" would be present.

Humming, Judah and Anna got together the graphs, charts, profiles and estimates for him to take to the Prentice home for the meeting with the "interested men." "Cloudy days will soon blow over," Judah told his ever patient wife.

The meeting was a small one. Mr. Prentice, the host, was present. So were W. H. Stoddard and Mark Hopkins, Huntington's business partner. Huntington asked all of the questions:

"What must be done first on the Dutch Flat route?"

"We must make an accurate instrument survey."

"How much will this survey cost?"

"Thirty-five thousand dollars is my estimate."

"How far will the survey go?"

"Approximately one hundred and fifteen miles to the Nevada line."

There were other questions and other answers. Mr. Hopkins, always against speculation, was in doubt, but Huntington said, "I will carry this survey through. I will not agree to do anything farther than that. I will bring in a group of six other businessmen to join me in this enterprise."

The absolute assurance of the man amazed Judah, even as it filled him with confidence. As the men filed out Huntington stopped Judah. "As I said, you are going about this thing in the wrong way. You must first have funds to demonstrate the merits of your scheme and lay a substantial foundation, then the public will support it sufficiently to bring appropriations from state, national, county and city bodies as well as from

It was in the second floor rooms of the Huntington & Hopkins Hardware Store the decision was made to incorporate the Central Pacific Railroad Company. Later these same rooms would serve as the railroad's headquarters. — MARINERS MUSEUM

private capital."

The next day Huntington met Crocker on the street and stopped him for a moment. "Has Judah approached you about this railroad, Crocker?"

"He has. You appear to take an interest in it."

"Yes, I want to talk to you about it. We are trying to form a syndicate and your name has been favorably mentioned."

Now Charles Crocker knew which way the cat would jump. "Well, I think anything you and Uncle Mark undertake is worthy of attention."

There was a second railroad meeting, this time not in the St. Charles Hotel but in the room above the Huntington-Hopkins Hardware Store. The very place of the meeting gave it status. Judah sat at a table with his data, his pamphlets, profiles, sketches and estimates spread out before him. He had sent for his friend, Doctor Strong, who had hurried in by stage and now scarcely concealed his excitement and eagerness. He had also specially invited the young surveyor, Mr. Fleete, who would no doubt help with the instrument survey when it was begun, and James Bailey, Judah's rich jeweler friend who had promised to "come in" when the right time came. Bailey had strange eyes, sometimes brown, sometimes gray, sometimes almost golden. Later Huntington called him "Old Calico Eyes." These eyes were fixed on Judah with warm encouragement. Others present were Cornelius Cole, who later became United States Senator from California; Lucius Booth with whom Judah had talked innumerable times; John Marsh of Nevada City; Charles Crocker who sold dry goods; Leland Stanford, a wholesale grocer and already a power in state politics; Huntington, the host, and his partner, "Uncle" Mark Hopkins, who were in the hardware business.

Judah knew all of these men, as who wouldn't if he had lived in Sacramento; but Crocker, Stanford, Huntington and Hopkins had never been personal friends.

Perhaps the strangest man in the group was Mark Hopkins, Huntington's business partner and like Huntington a '49er. Sacramento was a young man's town and Hopkins, born in 1813 at Henderson, New York, seemed an old man at 49. He looked old, too, because he was so thin, sad faced, slightly bent and

Quiet Mark Hopkins was a man of mystery — a mystery that has
never been solved and perhaps never will be. He was scrupulous
in detail and accuracy but limited in vision and imagination.
He often acted as a brake on the enthusiasm of the others. —
SOUTHERN PACIFIC COLLECTION

quiet. He had a long thin nose on a long thin face that grew a long thin beard. "He loved horses, dogs and book-keeping" and didn't care much for most people. When he spoke everybody listened carefully to hear him; even then his decided lisp sometimes made his words hard to understand. As others spoke he stroked his scraggly whisk broom of a beard with a long, thin, sallow hand. How did he and Huntington happen to be in business together? Why did Huntington rely on the judgment of this shadow of a man who was scrupulous to detail and accuracy but whose vision was limited, or so it seemed, by a bookkeeper's mind?

Sitting next to Hopkins, and in strange contrast with him, was the bulky, vigorous, loud-mouthed Charles Crocker. California was filled with self-made men: two of these were Leland Stanford and Collis P. Huntington, but Crocker had lived the roughest life. He had been entirely self-supporting since he was ten. At ten Huntington had been working on his father's farm, Stanford on his father's woodlot, and Judah, living in a pleasant, understanding home, had been preparing to enter the classic course at the Institute. Crocker, his father a so-so saloon keeper, was fighting for a place to sell papers on the roughest dock in New York State. When he was twelve he went in debt $200 to buy a newspaper agency when his father and four older brothers had taken a canal boat up the Erie to locate a homesite southeast of Chicago in Indiana. To pay back the money and to support his mother and sister, Charles quit school and gave all of his time to the newspaper agency.

At twelve Charles was a coarse-muscled, oversized boy with hard, fast fists and a voice like a bull, from which he probably got his nickname. He held his place among the peddlers at the ferry and railroad terminal by courage and willingness to defend it. But he grew tired of this work with no future in it. With money he had saved he took his sister and mother out to his father in Indiana. He went to work grubbing out tree trunks and roots to make farmland. There began at once a power struggle between him and his father. His father wanted to give the orders and have the orders obeyed without question. Charles had been on his own too long to give this sort of obedience to anyone. He considered working for his father nothing

Charles Crocker was loud, profane, stubborn, tactless, proud of making people fear him; but he was an indefatigable worker and would be the man who actually "built" the Central Pacific Railroad. — SOUTHERN PACIFIC COLLECTION

but slavery.

When he was seventeen he threw down his hoe and asked his father, "Father, do you *want* me to leave home?"

His father answered, "Yes, and no. Yes, because you are of no use to me here. No, because I am afraid you would starve among strangers." Charles paid no attention to his father's words. He knew well enough that his father was incapable of looking at him with fair eyes, that he would never starve, anywhere. He was born to be a leader, not a slave.

For a time he worked for a farmer, then for a millowner, then he started across the plains, one of the original "forty-niners." And in any company in which he travelled, though he was just a young man, he was a leader. Later he wrote, "They would all gather around me and want to know what to do." He learned that if a man assumes leadership he is accepted as a leader. "You've got to put your own price on your head if you want other people to pay it." He never used his leadership to get out of physical work. He loved it and always plunged into it. "I was always the one to swim a river and carry the rope across."

With an older brother he opened a store in Eldorado and in 1852 he had saved enough to go back East and marry Mary Deming, who was the daughter of the sawmill owner who had given Charles a job when he needed it. As soon as he returned to California he opened a drygoods business in Sacramento.

Sitting across from Judah he more than filled a stout chair. He weighed more than 250 pounds. Judah could understand railroads, financing, mountains, surveys, materials, but he never could understand men like "Bull" Crocker. Crocker was loud, profane, stubborn, tactless, proud of himself and what he had accomplished, and yet he had a good side, too. You could trust Charlie Crocker, everybody said that. He never claimed to be what he wasn't. He wasn't cunning nor shrewd. Once he said, "One man works hard all his life and ends up a pauper. Another man, no smarter, makes twenty million dollars. Luck has a hell of a lot to do with it."

Of the men that Huntington had invited to the meeting the one of whom Judah had heard the most was Leland Stanford, the dark, heavy-faced man sitting at Huntington's left. Stan-

101

Leland Stanford, later Governor of California and President of the Central Pacific Railroad, loved being in the public eye. It was he who handled the political problems of the Central Pacific Railroad project. — SOUTHERN PACIFIC COLLECTION

ford was high in State politics. He was an outstanding Republican and everybody said that he would be the next governor of California.

Leland Stanford was born March 9, 1824, near Albany, New York. His father, Josiah, was a tavern keeper at the Bull's Head Tavern near the ferry dock on the Hudson's Watervliet shore. When Leland was just six years old the railroad changed his life. The Mohawk & Hudson was being built across the Albany Schnectady plateau and his father deserted the tavern for a grand speculation. Josiah borrowed money and bought the Elm Grove Hotel, a half way house on the route. The big thing about the deal was that the hotel stood on three hundred acres of wooded land. The locomotives at that time were all woodburners. Josiah could see his seven sons cutting all of that wood which could be sold directly to the railroad. At first Leland carried or dragged the wood which his brothers cut to the place where it was sawed and corded. Soon he learned to handle the ax and the saw.

As a young boy he was overfat and very plain. He had a long jaw, deepset eyes, big ears that stood out from his head like the handles on a jug, and he faced life with an emotionless stare. He had little to say to anybody. In his family the boys worked rather than talked. Perhaps because he was dominated and ordered around by his older brothers he never spoke unless he was asked a direct question and then he answered slowly and deliberately as if the answer had come from his inner depths. It may have been slow boiling anger at his brother's bossiness that made him a man who longed for power and domination. This desire led him, most naturally, into politics as soon as he arrived in California in 1852. In nine years he had climbed up through minor offices to the favored head of his party. He had tried for governor unsuccessfully but he expected to try again now that the Republicans were the favored party.

Since Huntington, too, was a Republican, it might have been this political bond that brought him the invitation to the meeting.

When he had brought his wife out via the Isthmus she had been violently seasick all of the way. He had told her gently, "I will build a railroad one of these days for you to go back on."

But perhaps at the time of the meeting with Judah no one knew about this promise but his wife.

Judah could not know what was going on in Stanford's mind, nor in Huntington's. Stanford, he had heard, liked to be conspicuous. Huntington didn't. Instead of speaking at Judah's railroad meeting he had remained quiet and seemingly disinterested and then had spoken a few quiet words to Judah entirely in private. He liked to control things from behind a screen — a human screen. Perhaps he had already selected Stanford to "front" for him. Perhaps he had in mind railroad legislation which would be helpful to any new road and with an interested governor who was also a "railroad man" that would not be impossible to secure. The really important man who faced Judah from across the table was Collis P. Huntington.

"Old Huntington," as he was called in Sacramento, was not yet 40. He was born in Harwinton, Connecticut, in 1821, which made him just five years older than Judah. At fourteen he ran away from home and hired out as a farm hand. The work was hard because he was expected to do all that a full grown man could do and accept much less pay. He saved every dime he earned and at the end of the year he had $84.00. While he had been doing the back-breaking work he had dreamed a dream of high finance. He used the $84.00 to go to Oneonta, New York, via Albany. In Oneonta he became a grocery clerk, and living with incredible frugality he again saved almost all of his salary. It took him twelve years of saving before he had enough to buy a quantity of goods that would sell well in California and have it shipped around the Horn.

The goods left in the fall of 1848 and in 1849 he went by way of the Isthmus, travelling on the S.S. *Crescent City*, lowest class.

The Isthmus stop was at Chagres, a shabby collection of primitive huts, frowned on from a cliff by the Castle of San Lorenzo, built by Philip of Spain in the 16th century. In Chagres there were tropical and humid temperatures and there were torrential rains. Anybody who landed there risked getting yellow fever, malaria, cholera. From the ship's deck Huntington gazed up at the fortress. He had no use for kings but he was interested in the power and money that went with kingship. He took a small boat from the ship that was anchored on the

Collis P. Huntington was a financial genius. He had worked his
way up from poverty and he knew the value of money. Huntington would be the financial brains of the railroad corporation. –

seaward side of the Laja Reefs and in spite of warnings went to shore.

Ordinarily there was a charge of $30 for each passenger to make the trip up the river to Gargona or Cruces in native boats called *cayucas* that were made from hollowing out tree trunks. Huntington set up a bargain. He could promise 1,000 passengers if the natives would carry them for $7.00 apiece. The natives accepted the bargain. Huntington went back to the *Crescent City* and offered the passengers the trip up the river for $10.00 each. He kept $3.00 out of each fare to pay for horses or pack mules to carry the passengers from Gorgona to Panama City, a distance of twenty miles. Since he also bargained with muleteers who took passengers along the narrow bridle path, he had money left over.

Panama City was in a beautiful location, but it was as dangerous a place as Chagres with cholera, dysentery, yellow fever. And the travellers from the *Crescent City* had arrived too late for the packet with which they were supposed to make connections. There would be a three months wait.

There was a ship travelling south from Panama City and some of the wealthier travellers waiting there took passage to a South American coastal town where they got quicker passage to San Francisco. The others were miserable in Panama City. Every day there were eight or ten deaths. But Huntington didn't wait to be caught by the fever. With the money he had earned on the across-the-Isthmus deal he bought some donkeys and worked at transferring freight and baggage across the Isthmus in competition with the native mule drivers. He walked the twenty miles from Panama City to Gorgona and back twelve times. With the money he earned from this freighting business and from the sale of the donkeys he had bought to conduct it, he left for Bogota on foot. It was 30 miles to Bogota and he walked these 30 miles under a blazing tropical sun and said he had never felt better in his life. In Bogota he bought a boat, the *Emma,* loaded her with rice, potatoes, flour, sugar, dried beef and sailed her to Panama where he sold both the boat and the supplies at a profit.

At this time he was described as a "sunshiny companion when skies were cloudy and seas were rough. He was a genial young man and everybody liked him."

Three months had passed since the *Crescent City* had anchored off the Laja Reefs and at last a steamer bound for San Francisco put in at Panama. Huntington could have purchased first class fare for $300 but instead he took the cheapest ticket, $100. He arrived in San Francisco August 30, 1849. He had travelled 2,500 miles from New York to the Chagres River, sixty miles across the Isthmus, 3,500 miles from Panama to San Francico. He had left New York with $1,200 in cash. He arrived in San Francisco with $5,000.

While all of the other men were rushing off to try their luck at finding gold on river banks and sand bars he opened a business in Sacramento, setting out his goods under a big tent made of old sails that he had bought at a bargain. Soon he opened up a team service to convey men and their supplies to the various mining camps and his store spread to fill five tents. In Sacramento, though he was not yet thirty, he was called "Old Huntington." He had a business motto: "Anything that can be bought for less than production, is not perishable, and is an article in use is worth buying and holding."

He slept in his store, didn't waste money on smoking, drinking nor gambling, never sold goods for just a fair profit but charged as much as he could get, and never gave anything away. Once he said of himself, "I'll never be remembered for the money I've given away." And much later, "Young man, you can't follow me through life by the quarters I've dropped." Even after he brought his wife out they lived on the upper floor of the 54 K Street store. It was much later when he built an unpretentious dwelling at M Street between 3rd and 4th.

Everybody on the streets of Sacramento knew how sharp a businessman Huntington was. The storytellers of the town seemed to take a pride in telling tales of Huntington's shrewdness, all true. Judah must have heard these stories. Two of the favorites were the blasting powder story and the story of the tent.

Once Huntington and Hopkins bought up all the available blasting powder. Miners had to have blasting powder no matter how much it cost, so they paid Huntington and Hopkins thousands of dollars. One day two men came into the store with a used tent they wanted to sell. Huntington bought it at the lowest price they would take. Then he put up the tent and fastened a sign to it: *For Sale.* Courteously he invited the former owners to sit under it until time to catch their stage. While they were still sitting under the tent Huntington sold it for five times what he had paid for it.

Yet Judah was not uncomfortable about Huntington's shrewdness; rather he was complimented that Huntington would find his estimates workable and be willing to come into the enterprise. Truly, if Huntington thought the railroad a good deal it must be.

Judah looked at Huntington with his proud eyes, his thin, tightly drawn lips, his small ears laid flat against his skull; at the heavy, dark, impassive face of Leland Stanford; at the coarse, ruddy, open face of Charles Crocker; at Uncle Mark Hopkins' face, almost covered by the skinny hand until the hand was brought slowly downward grasping the limp beard. He looked at the four and made a mistake. These men, he decided, were not like the financiers he had addressed in San Francisco. They were not dreamers, visionaries, idealists; they were shopkeepers. He showed his profiles, his estimates, his maps, just as he had planned to do, but now he spoke to them not of the transcontinental span he dreamed of, but of the opportunity of controlling the markets of the mining towns in Nevada. "It is purely local; you are tradesmen of Sacramento City; your property, your business is here. Help me to make the survey. I will make you the company. And with the bill passed you will have control of business interests that will make your fortunes in trade if nothing more. Why, you can have a wagon road if not a railroad."

"You can have a wagon road if not a railroad." Later he didn't want to hear these words repeated.

Uncle Mark, with his skinny hand still caressing his skinny beard said, "That looks to me like a great mountain that offers a vast amount of work."

EIGHT

The Big Four
and the Central Pacific

THE MEN STAYED late at 54 K Street. Before the meeting was over Huntington, Hopkins, Stanford and Crocker as well as James Bailey, had each subscribed for 150 shares in the Central Pacific Railroad Company soon to be incorporated. Judah was to have 150 shares, too, but he wouldn't put up any money since he had already paid for his shares many times over by the time and money he had spent in working in behalf of the railroad. The agreement was not written down. Huntington explained that verbal agreements were the style in Sacramento and he, Huntington, liked agreements that way. Judah, who had dreamed railroad since he was a boy and who had put building a railroad above every personal consideration, was now linked with Huntington, Crocker, Stanford and Hopkins who from their childhood had been forced by their hard lives to put themselves and their personal interests above everything else. It was a strange, even dangerous arrangement, but Judah was jubilant.

At the Vernon house where the Judahs had taken rooms, Anna was waiting up for him. "Anna," he said, "the door has opened up for us!" He told Anna of everything that had happened in the upper room of the Huntington-Hopkins hardware store and when she didn't share his excitement he said, "Anna, don't you understand? With these men backing me there will be more than enough subscribed to incorporate under the law. I shall be able to put the name of the Central Pacific Railroad Company in the Railroad Bill when it is presented to Congress." Anna had heard stories about the way that at least two of these men had always done business in Sacramento and she may have wished that the agreement had not been verbal, but she had confidence in her husband.

Each of the men had put in $50 out of his pocket to commence a railroad survey on Sacramento's Front Street that would follow up the American River. A few days later, when Judah rose from the breakfast table he said, "Anna, if you want to see the first work done on the Pacific Railroad, look out of your bedroom window. I am going to work this morning and I am going to have these men pay for it."

She answered almost wearily, "I'm glad, Theodore. It's about time somebody else helped."

Anna watched the survey begun on Front Street. Judah and surveyor assistants with chains and stakes and heavy instruments drew a crowd of gawking spectators to the muddy street. Though it was January the weather was clear and warm enough for the survey to progress as far as Dutch Flat before the first of March. In March there was a spell of inclement weather that stopped the survey and sent Judah home to Sacramento.

Never one to be idle, Judah decided to interest the general public in the railroad. From his experience with the Central Pacific Museum in Washington he had learned the value of dramatizing the railroad. Perhaps he had known this intuitively since he with L. L. Robinson and the others had lifted the hand car onto the Sacramento Valley tracks and had taken the first ride by rail in California. Now he visualized a railroad structure in Sacramento that would serve as an office building and also a museum with a public display of ores, minerals, fossils, charts, maps, profiles, sketches, paintings — all of the exhibits which had attracted so much interest in Washington — that would incite general interest in the project and make people feel that a railroad was actually going to be built eastward across the mountains. He drew up careful plans for the building, which he estimated would cost $12,000.

When he presented his ideas to Stanford and Huntington, Stanford gave the matter careful consideration and nodded his head in agreement. Huntington took a piece of paper and drew a freehand plan for a small wooden shack that could be built in a day for $150. He handed his drawing to Judah.

"But this will not do at all," Judah exclaimed, remembering the hundreds of people who had filed through the Washington exhibit. "Selling a railroad to the people is not like selling ten penny nails."

Without a word Huntington gave Judah the careful plan of the $12,000 building and walked away. Judah was insulted and frustrated. It was the first time in his long effort to "start the ball rolling" that he had felt so furious and so helpless.

Huntington's shanty was built, tossed up in a day and for $150. For some time it served as office and station. Soon railroad offices were opened on the second floor of 56-58 K Street, unused rooms above the Stanford Grocery Store. Later, when these two rooms were outgrown, a door was cut through to the second story of 54 K Street where the first meeting had been held. Huntington's shack ended its life as a shed for storing paint.

Since Judah had left Washington, ominous things had been happening. In 1860 General Scott, "Old Fuss and Feathers," had been recalled to Washington. He was a grand figure of a glorious warrior — deteriorated by age. In 1814 he had defeated the British, in 1848 he had defeated the Mexicans. Now, in 1860, he could no longer sit a horse and arrived in Washington by carriage. Once he had been six feet four and one quarter with an emphasis on the one quarter; now he stooped as he walked, leaning on the arm of an aide. He had opposed Franklin Pierce for the Presidency eight years before and had been defeated. Definitely his good days were over. With the United States Army small, at best, and what there was of it deployed to fight Indians in the West or to guard Utah Territory, which never had been and never would be in rebellion, he was expected to look ahead for the protection of Washington and the preservation of the Union.

If Maryland and Virginia seceded (and congressmen and

If one exempts the office at the Huntington & Hopkins Hardware Store, the first structure on the Central Pacific was this unpainted shack by the riverbank in Sacramento. It served as the railroad's first passenger station, division headquarters, supply base and executive office. Later it was a tool house and still later a storage shed for paint. — SOUTHERN PACIFIC COLLECTION

three of the President's cabinet — Cobb of Georgia, Secretary of the Treasury; Floyd of Virginia, Secretary of War; and Thompson of Mississippi, Secretary of the Interior — as well as many clerks were openly wearing secession cockades in their buttonholes) Washington, D.C., would fall like a ripe plum. Lincoln was elected in November and all of his talk of saving the Union was considered just so much talk. In December South Carolina seceded and on Christmas day the *Richmond Examiner* called for Maryland to join Virginia in seizing the capital. After the first break secession came fast: Mississippi, Alabama, Georgia, Louisiana and Texas. South Carolina guns had fired on the Union flag and had driven off *Star of the West* when it attempted to reinforce Fort Sumter without arousing much indignation in Washington.

Judah knew that now there would be no reluctance to consider a railroad bill in Congress for fear that a discussion of whether the railroad should take a southern or a central route would make a wider breach between the North and South. By the time Judah returned from Dutch Flat to Sacramento in March, that breach was already as wide as it could ever be. Southern Congressmen had left their seats and Southern Senators, many of them giving impassioned farewell addresses, had left the Senate to take over positions of importance in the new Confederacy.

In California, especially in San Francisco, there was a strong secessionist movement, but most of the people of California desired to see the Union preserved, though there was no strong anti-slavery feeling. A railroad that followed the Mormon Trail-Donner Pass route would tie the Union together. Gold could flow to the North that needed it so badly. It was conceivable that a railroad could save the Union, since men and supplies could be gathered all through the West where the cause of freedom was a part of the pioneer spirit. People began to talk of the railroad as if it were already built or could be built in a few months' time. Judah and his associates didn't discourage this optimism. They were all strong Republicans and Leland Stanford was later to be known as a friend of Lincoln and one of the great wartime governors.

On April 13, Fort Sumter was surrendered and on April 30

Mark Hopkins called a meeting of the railroad's principal stockholders.

At this April 30 meeting the Central Pacific Railroad Company was organized. The company was capitalized at $8,500,-000 and its stated purpose was to construct a railroad from Sacramento to the eastern boundary of the state, a distance of about 115 miles. For that distance more than $1,000 a mile had been subscribed and ten percent had already been paid in as the law required. Articles of Association were adopted, officers and a board of directors were elected, and a board of commissioners was appointed. The officers were Leland Stanford, who loved to be before the public and made a magnificent and dignified appearance, president; Collis P. Huntington, who loved to be out of sight but in a position to control, vice president; Mark Hopkins, who loved the keeping of books and was meticulous and honest, treasurer; and James Bailey, secretary. James Bailey, the only one of Judah's close associates to hold office, had the least important position. The board of directors included all of the officers plus Charles Crocker, Lucius Booth, Doctor Daniel Strong, Charles Marsh, and John F. Morse.

Judah's friend, James Bailey, may have been the richest man in the group though word on Front Street was that Collis P. Huntington had blown his original $1,000 to one million. (Much later, Leland Stanford was to make a sworn statement that in 1862 the combined fortunes of Huntington, Hopkins, Crocker and himself was less than $125,000.) Marsh lived in Nevada City where he had interests in mines and water companies. Lucius Booth had a large grocery store on J Street in Sacramento. All of them, with the exception of Doctor Strong, were men of means. But Strong was a man of practical ideas in whom his patients over a wide area had absolute confidence. Yet it appeared later that Huntington expected the board of directors to rubber stamp the policies which he, himself, would originate. Judah had no voice in the direction of the company. He was *Chief Engineer,* and he thought his position plus his recognized ability would give him absolute direction of engineering problems, which, after all, were the problems in which he had the greatest interest.

There were smaller stockholders, too, who had no voice in

policy making. Two held fifty shares; one, forty; two, twenty-five; one, twenty; twelve, ten; six, five. Of the 1,250 shares 900 were held by six men. Huntington considered the small stockholders merely "investors."

On June 10, Leland Stanford was nominated for Governor of California on the Republican ticket, a nomination that almost assured election. On June 28, the company of which he was president applied for incorporation papers and filed its certificate of incorporation in the office of the Secretary of State in Sacramento. No one thought that it was unusual for these two events to take place in the same month.

Already the company had printed handsome stock certificates with Anna's sketches of Donner Lake and Donner Pass engraved on them. The stock was to be sold by the appointed commissioners. Samuel Brannan, a San Francisco capitalist, immediately became the largest stockholder, with 200 shares, but the officers, firmly entrenched in the original organization, never gave him a voice in policy making. He, too, was an "investor." The policy makers were to be Huntington, Hopkins and Stanford.

Judah soon discovered that even his engineering decisions were to be questioned. He was certain that the Dutch Flat-Donner Pass route was the only feasible route, but the board of directors, all but James Bailey, agreeing with Huntington who knew nothing of surveying, decided to resurvey all five possible routes. A waste of time and money, Judah protested. He thought it much wiser to build a toll road at once. Earnings from the road carrying supplies and men to the mines and ore from them would pay for this road which they would need to carry men and materials to grade the railroad line. The wagon road should be built over the Dutch Flat-Donner Pass route, of course. He had been over all the routes with his instruments and could furnish profiles and general estimates. Some of the roads he had not worked on completely because when the topography made planning a railroad over it impossible he had dropped the survey.

Huntington, Charles Marsh and Congressman-elect A. A. Sargent, who planned to present a railroad bill in Congress, went with Judah to check the Feather River route. They hiked down the middle fork of the Feather River to the neighborhood of Nelson's Bar where the canyon cut by the river commenced. Huntington insisted that this might be the best route. Sargent and Marsh gave up and returned to Sacramento, but Huntington and Judah continued the exploration. Huntington was a giant mentally and physically, and he had matching endurance, but it was Judah who knew the best ways to skirt a granite out-cropping and inch his way up the face of a sheer cliff. The two men took a Chinaman along to help them carry provisions and blankets. For seven days they worked their way through Nelson's Canyon to Bidwell Bar, a distance of 70 miles through granite, slate and marble. According to an article in the *Sacramento Union*, the walls rose two to three thousand feet, cut through on an "extremely crooked line with angles of every variety." Judah estimated that at least 30, probably 40, tunnels would be required if the railroad followed this route and the road would have to be blasted out of solid rock most of the way. The miners who lived above the canyon said they descended into the canyon with ropes when they needed water and that as far as they knew no human being had ever attempted the exploration before. What was even more important, some of them declared that the water had risen 70 feet in the narrow canyon only the year before. The distance would be 65 miles longer than the Donner Pass route.

Huntington, having experienced the troubles of the route himself, voted with the board of directors when it declared that this route was not feasible.

Judah insisted that work be begun on the Dutch Flat-Donner Lake route but the board, once more expressing Huntington's will, voted to study the other possibilities before making the instrument survey of the road that Judah already knew was the least expensive and best.

Much of the time that Judah was in the mountains making these surveys Anna was with him. She was concerned about his health, eager to look after him. When the survey of the Donner Pass route was underway she added to her pencil sketches while he and the other surveyors drove stakes at 100-foot intervals marking out what Judah called a "side hill" line which kept close to the tops of the successive ridges but stayed on the north slope. He estimated that eighteen tunnels would be needed and most of these would not exceed 1,000 feet. He decided that the best way to reach the valley floor at Donner Lake was to slant down the steep north slopes of the mountains that formed a rim south of the lake's basin. After the line reached the Truckee River all of the difficult problems would be behind them. The river flowed toward the Nevada line at an easy pitch that the railroad could follow. The measured distance from Sacramento to Truckee was 123 miles, to the Nevada border, 145 miles. Judah had been 30 miles short on his estimate.

Judah knew that there would be snow problems 8,000 feet above sea level, but since he had had little experience with snow he didn't give the problem enough consideration. He said that since the line would lie high on a shelf etched out of the mountain, the snow would simply slide off. When Judah made a mistake he made a "whopper," but he always erred on the side of optimism.

By August Judah was ready to make his preliminary report on all of the completed surveys. He was ready to list the difficulties and problems that would be encountered. He was optimistic about solving the problems on the Dutch Flat-Donner Pass route and claimed it had at least 30 advantages over the others. Although the western slope of the mountain was rugged in the extreme and there was a 7,000-foot rise in less than 20 miles, the proposed route crossed no deep rivers or canyons or gorges. The longest tunnel would not exceed 1,350 feet.

Reporting to the board of directors he said: "It commands and will perform the entire business of Nevada Territory, Washoe and the silver mine region. It will also command the business of the newly discovered Humboldt Mineral District, Pyramid Lake, Esmeralda and Monomineral districts. It will reduce the time of passenger transit to or from Washoe to eight and one half hours. The citizens of the mining region will save a million dollars a year on their freight bill alone by using the new railroad. It will make possible the shipping of low grade ore which is now heaped uselessly about three thousand tunnel heads." And he finished by saying, "The line over the mountains completes the first Western link of the Pacific Railroad, overcoming its greatest difficulties."

The board of directors still was not satisfied and Doctor Strong and James Bailey as well as Judah grew annoyed with these storekeepers who set themselves up as judges of railroad routes. Huntington, Stanford, and Crocker went over the route though Crocker declared he didn't know anything about railroads. They were none of them engineers but they carefully explored the route, discussing difficulties and estimating profits. Huntington, who had never worked on a railroad in his life, nor in any type of construction, assured Judah that Judah's plans called for too much earthwork and not enough rock.

Even though Judah felt that resurvey of the routes he had already found impossible was a waste of time and energy and money at a time when all three could be put to better use, it was a relief to him that the board of directors had taken over the task of raising money so that he could spend all of his time in actual engineering. From April until the directors' meeting in October the greatest concern of the officers was to find available investors. Judah's lowest estimate for the cost of building to the Nevada border was $12,380,000. The stockholders simply didn't have that kind of money. Judah had felt when he had been in Washington pushing his earlier railroad bill of '59-'60 that the transcontinental line should be built by private capital and that the government should agree to guarantee interest on investments so that private capital could be induced to invest. He had felt that certainly private capital and state and county governments in California could build the line to the Nevada border. Now he began to change his mind. It seemed that government aid was the only answer to financial needs. William Tecumseh Sherman in 1857 had called the building of the transcontinental railroad the "work of giants" and declared that "Uncle Sam is the only Giant I know who can grapple with the subject."

Judah spent all of August and part of September working at his table, mapping surveys, making profiles, gathering all sorts of information into the graphs. In October he had a complete report on estimated distances and costs ready. (The route suggested in this report is almost the one followed by the Central Pacific, which is now the Southern Pacific Overland Route.)

The estimates of cost were as follows:

Sacramento to the State line	140 miles	$12,380,000
State line to Salt Lake Cty	593 miles	$29,035,000
Total	733 miles	$41,415,000
Council Bluffs to Salt Lake City	1,125 miles	$58,000,000
Total	1,858 miles	$99,870,000

Judah had already discovered that it was not easy to interest capital on the Coast. Even though Huntington, Hopkins and Stanford were well known as shrewd businessmen they found it almost as difficult. Perhaps their reputation as businessmen made it even more difficult. People couldn't imagine any one of the three as being unselfish visionaries who were doing this great thing for the public good.

There were many who wanted the railroad to fail. The telegraph company, which had almost completed its lines across the country, saw a rival, as did the Pacific Mail, Wells Fargo Company, the Sacramento Valley Railroad and all of the stage lines. They acted together to make it difficult for the Central Pacific Company to find purchasers for its beautiful stock certificates. Bankers told those who asked for advice, and many who didn't, "Don't have anything to do with these men, Stanford, Huntington, Hopkins and Crocker. Don't put your money into their schemes. They are bound to come to grief. Nobody in this world can put that road through."

Perhaps if there had been a Central Pacific Railroad Museum in Sacramento as there had been in Washington, investors could have seen for themselves that such a road was not only desirable but possible. But $12,000 had been saved by setting up offices in an unused attic.

On October 9, the board of directors passed the following resolution:

Resolved that Mr. T. D. Judah, the Chief Engineer of this Company, proceed to Washington on the steamer of the 11th October inst. as the accredited agent of the Central Pacific Railroad Company of California for the purpose of procuring appropriations of land and U. S. Bonds from the government to aid in the construction of the road.

Judah was eager to get to Washington. This time he had a corporation behind him, he had made an instrument survey of a feasible route and there were no questions about the projected road that he could not answer. The time was ripe for the building of the road. Surely he could not fail again.

Once again Anna found the right gaiters. The luggage, including all of Judah's precious materials and Anna's sketches, was on the pier two days later, on the eleventh of October.

NINE

The Railroad Bill of 1862

HOPE BURNED high in the Judahs, in their friend James Bailey, who had decided to accompany them East, and in Congressman-elect Aaron Sargent as their ship sailed out through the Golden Gate. Now, Judah thought, all of our worries are behind us. Aaron Sargent had accompanied Judah and Huntington on a part of their exploration of the Feather River route so he and Judah were more than acquaintances. Judah, Bailey and Sargent, sharing the same paramount interest, spent long hours talking railroad and working out the exact wording of the bill that would provide for the building of the transcontinental line and put the California section, at least, in the hands of their company. Ever since Judah had interested the Sacramento storekeepers, later called the *Big Four*, in his railroad project, he had pressed them to also incorporate in Nevada. The Company could then build over the flat terrain of Nevada as well as over the mountains of California. If this incorporation were completed before the bill they were formulating was presented to Congress, the wording could be changed so as to give the Central Pacific Railroad Company the right to build eastward to Utah.

Congressman-elect Sargent was preparing to present the bill in the House. Judah should have remembered that Congressman Burch as a freshman congressman had been unable to get even a hearing in the House. He probably put this problem out of his mind as he did many negative things.

Before the ship reached Panama the first transcontinental telegraph line was open. Now messages from the East to the West or from the West to the East did not have to depend upon overland stage or Pony Express. When the ship docked in New York Judah received a telegram stating that the Central Pacific Railroad Company had formed a "paper company" and had organized and incorporated the Nevada Rail Road Company under Nevada legislation which authorized the company to construct a railroad across Nevada, a distance of 275 miles. The Big Four, Judah and Bailey were all equal incorporators with $10,000 in stock credited to each. The act under which the railroad was incorporated read:

"An act granting certain persons the right to construct a railroad from the Western to the Eastern boundary of Nevada."

This bill was signed by the Governor of Nevada November 25, 1861, the day the Judahs arrived in New York.

The Judahs, Bailey and Sargent were jubilant, but their spirits were soon depressed by the concern in New York about the progress of the war, by the disruption of life that is felt near the battleground. On the California Coast the war had seemed remote in spite of a strong secessionist movement that had been fostered by such strong pro-slavery men as Senator Gwin.

In 1859 Gwin, the Senator who had proposed a survey of three railroad routes across the continent so that work could begin on none of them and had refused to give the Central Pacific Railroad his support, had spoken his convictions in the Senate:

"I say that a dissolution of the Union is not impossible, that it is not impracticable, and that the northern states are laboring under a delusion if they think that the southern states cannot separate from them either violently or peaceably, violently if necessary."

Senator Gwin, who had come to California with the purpose

of being elected Senator, had served pro-slavery interests rather than the interests of California all of the time he was in the Senate. In California he tried unsuccessfully to split the state.

The first shot in the conflict between anti-slavery and pro-slavery sympathizers was also fired in 1859. California's other Senator, David Broderick, as anti-slavery as Gwin was pro-slavery, was tactless, strong and incorruptible and dedicated to the working man. In 1859 he was forced into a duel with Chief Justice Terry. Broderick recognized the maneuver for what it was, an attempt to get rid of him as the anti-slavery leader. At first he refused to meet Justice Terry but when the Justice resigned his position and challenged Broderick in a series of insulting letters, he finally took up the challenge. He was an expert shot yet Terry, who preferred the bowie knife, consented to the use of pistols.

The two men met on the sand dunes south of San Francisco. The pistols were presented and Terry, who had allowed Broderick to name the kind of weapon, had his choice of the two pistols. Rumor said that he had studied both pistols beforehand and knew which one to select. The men stood back to back, walked off ten paces, faced each other, raised their revolvers. Broderick's went off before he had had time to aim and he didn't touch the trigger. Terry aimed and shot Broderick through the left breast. The revolver Terry had left for Broderick had a "hair trigger so light and delicate that the pistol would discharge on a sudden jar or motion without touching the trigger." Three days later David Broderick died saying, "They have killed me because I was opposed to the extension of slavery." In San Francisco business houses closed, 30,000 people assembled in the plaza where his body rested on a catafalque and listened to a eulogy that made David Broderick a martyr to the cause of the Union and strengthened and united the anti-slavery, anti-secessionist movement.

Still the affairs of California had been largely controlled by men of Southern sympathies. In 1860 not only Senator Gwin but Senator Latham was in favor of secession. Secret secessionist societies, "Knights of the Golden Circle," were organized with 18,000 members. After Lincoln was elected, the organization was no longer secret but flew palmetto flags. To combat the influence of the Knights of the Golden Circle, Union sympathizers organized and 40,000 paraded in San Francisco, marching behind martial bands.

Senator Gwin had used his influence to have Albert Sidney Johnston made commander of all the military forces in the state. Johnston, who was soon to be an army officer in the Confederacy, closed his eyes to the arming of the Knights. On April 24, 1861, Johnston was replaced with General E. A. Sumner, a Unionist. Sumner brought troops to San Francisco from Oregon and from Fort Mojave to Los Angeles. The secessionist movement was an urban movement with incidents reported in El Monte, San Bernardino, and Santa Barbara.

After the union defeat at Bull Run the Unionists in San Francisco sent this frightened message to the Secretary of War: "About three eighths of our citizens are natives of slave holding states and are almost a unit in this crisis."

Even with the secessionist movement strong in the cities, even with the news of the firing on Fort Sumter in April and the series of defeats suffered by the Union in the first months of the war, on the West Coast the war seemed almost like a fantasy with the wide continent between the East and the West.

Always Anna went directly to her family in Greenfield. If there had been any thought that she might stay in Washington with her husband it would have been dispelled at once by the situation in New York City. Everyone was talking about the debacle, of McDowell's Folly, of the inability of untrained troops, brave though they might be, to wage a successful war or even fight a successful battle. Just two weeks before Judah arrived in New York, General Winfield Scott had been replaced by General George, "Our George," McClellan, the thirty-five-year-old general who seemed to have youth, wisdom, vision, audacity and imagination but was later found to have only the first quality.

Judah, Bailey and Sargent hurried to Washington, arriving there just three months after the Union defeat at Bull Run.

Washington was no longer a Southern city with Negro slaves loitering in front of the fine hotels, with the lobbies and bars crowded with clerks and congressmen discussing the threatening disruption of the Union. Now it was an armed town, not exactly under siege, but constantly threatened. The city was guarded by brigades and surrounded by earthworks built at McClellan's insistence to release men for fighting. At the time the earthworks were thrown up McClellan was a subordinate to Scott, blaming every failure on his superior. Inside the town there seemed to be hundreds of soldiers and sashed officers. In the streets, at the bars, in the hotels there was a babble of foreign tongues, Italian, French, German. Professional soldiers of fortune, especially those from Garibaldi's Italian Army, had hurried across the Atlantic in hopes of becoming officers over the untrained recruits that were pouring into the army camps. It was known in Europe as well as in America that the expert soldiers were from the South, that the military tradition had been nurtured in the South and that the Union would have to make up in gold and courage for what it lacked in leadership.

In addition to the soldiers and would-be soldiers Washington was crowded with the usual camp-followers: contractors, builders, correspondents, relatives of dead or wounded soldiers who had come to seek information about their loved ones, counterfeiters, all sorts of confidence men, pickpockets, actors, singers, gay young women laughing and flirting in the company of the young officers, and on the side streets coarse women who accommodated anyone with a dollar in his pocket.

It was an ugly town, a disturbing town. Judah, with his strict Episcopalian background and his dedication to his dreams, felt repulsed, half sick. And yet he realized that if he could find his way in this confused situation the time might be ideal for pushing the railroad. Certainly the tension between the North and the South that had formerly been his chief obstacle had now erupted into war and so no longer existed.

Again in rented rooms he went to work to remap his campaign to fit this new Washington, this new world. The railroad should now be pushed as an urgent war measure, for Judah was as eager to serve the Union as to build the road. What if the Union army remained as inept as it had proven itself to be? What if General McClellan couldn't pull the forces together as he believed he could? Then the Union might lose California and Nevada. With a railroad the North would always be assured of a supply of gold and silver and grain from the West.

What if England, seeing the weakness of the Union, came to the aid of the Confederacy in revenge for her losses in the War of 1812? If England came into the war the British would almost certainly attack the practically defenseless West Coast. Without a railroad the country could not rush supplies, arms, and armies to California, Washington and Oregon.

All of these reasons for building the railroad might have seemed fantastic to anyone less enthusiastic than Judah, less frenzied than Union Congressmen and Senators, since the road could not be built in a day or a year. Yet people who had at first believed that the war was some sort of picnic and would be over in a couple of months now thought of it as being interminable, never ending.

What if the railroad weren't built until the war was over and paid for — perhaps thirty or forty years? A new generation would have grown up in California, a generation that felt no ties to the United States. Even though now every Californian spoke of some place "Back East" as "home," still withdrawal from the Union was not unthinkable. Judah's friend, Congressman Burch, thought that if the Union were divided California should become a separate republic and C. L. Scott, another California Congressman, had said, "If this Union is divided and two separate confederations are formed, I will strenuously advocate the secession of California and the establishment of a separate republic on the Pacific slopes."

Judah's first overt move was to reopen the Central Pacific Railroad Museum. It was not difficult to get permission to use the room in the Capitol and this year the exhibit was more complete than ever since it displayed the carefully surveyed route in maps and profiles, additional sketches and pictures by Anna and the beautiful stock certificate with the engravings of Donner Lake and Donner Pass. But now few people wandered into the Museum. The feeling of the times was against such quiet pursuits. There was much going on in the streets where the flamboyant McClellan could be counted on to stage a military review almost any day. People didn't want to talk to Judah about the continental railroad, they wanted to talk to each other about the war.

When Congress convened on the second of December Congressional attention had to be focused on the lack of progress in the War. The South was winning, there was no question about that. McClellan had refused to become the aggressor as long as he was the subordinate of Winfield Scott. Even after the old general was relieved of his command and taken to the railroad station by a disrespectful guard of honor, McClellan still refused to move. "All's quiet along the Potomac tonight" was an apt description of every night, and Congress appointed a committee to look into the conduct of the war. The Potomac had been blockaded, the Confederates had withdrawn from the front and McClellan didn't know where they were or what they were doing. The Union troops had been badly defeated at Ball's Bluff. There, Colonel E. D. Baker, who had left his seat in Congress to take an active place in the field, was killed because the military operation he engaged in had been so poorly planned that defeat was inevitable.

Even impatient Judah realized that Congress had to pass the legislation needed for military emergencies and do its usual routine work besides. Ordinarily the forming of necessary committees is not difficult, but with half of the seats vacant either because Confederates had occupied them or because Union members had gone into the battlefield, and with openings on every committee, movement was at a snail's pace. And yet it was this disorganization, this lack of suitable personnel, that finally gave Judah an unpredictable opportunity to work for his bill.

One day Sargent asked for the floor during a debate on another subject. He delivered a long and impassioned appeal for the railroad. The chairman appointed a subcommittee to consider the matter. Later a committee was appointed to study the Central Pacific Railroad, and still later a committee was appointed to consider the entire railroad problem.

James A. Dougall and Milton S. Latham, no longer proslavery in his attitude, were California's Senators. Sargent, Law and Timothy Phelps were Congressmen. Judah worked with these five and with other legislators he had met and influenced in his former winters in Washington, to get himself appointed Secretary of the Senate Committee on Pacific Railroads, Clerk of the House Committee on Pacific Railroads (this appointment

A. A. Sargent brought an impassioned appeal for a transcontinental railroad to the floor of the House of Representatives and thus set in motion the forces that made possible the Railroad Act of 1862. — CALIFORNIA STATE LIBRARY

was engineered by Aaron Sargent), and Clerk of the House Main Committee on Railroads. Never before or since has a lobbyist been so fortunate! He had access to all of the documents available to the committees, he had an opportunity to influence the thinking of committee members since they recognized him as an expert, he even had the privilege of speaking from the floor. In these positions he was practically able to write the bills in his own words and in his own way. Without his presence, experts think, the bills would probably never have been reported out of committee.

As soon as Judah was sure that there would be action on railroad legislation he wired the board of directors of the Central Pacific Railroad Company. Huntington had already wired that if matters looked favorable he would come to Washington. Now Judah's wire brought him hurrying. Huntington worked best face to face with one man at a time. His strategy was to call on each legislator personally, sizing up his man and presenting that aspect of the railroad most likely to interest him. Many of the legislators were businessmen and were impressed with the businessmen who had gone into the Central Pacific Railroad Company. Thaddeus Stevens of Pennsylvania, for example, was best persuaded to support the railroad when he was told of the benefit it would be to his iron producing constituents if the company bought all of its rails in the United States. Later Stevens was to declaim: "The Western Soil is but a platform on which to lay the rails to transport the wealth of the furthest Indies to Philadelphia, Boston, and Portland, scattering its benefits on its way to St. Louis, Chicago, Cincinnati, Buffalo and Albany. Then our Atlantic seaports will be but a resting place between China, Japan and Europe."

How much of this grandiose dream was borrowed from Huntington, how much was a paraphrase of Judah's words, and how much of it grew out of Stevens' love for oratory isn't known.

So Huntington worked with the legislators one by one in "the smoke-filled room" and Judah worked in the Congressional Committees. Yet, surprisingly, there were still some members of Congress who had never been in the Museum, who had never been approached directly about the actual progress of plans for the road. May 1, Samuel Shellbarger, representative from Ohio, offered an amendment to the railroad bill asking that surveys be made.

At last the bill, entitled "An Act to aid in the construction of a railroad and telegraph line from Missouri River to the Pacific Ocean . . . to secure the government use of the same for postal, military and other purposes" was reported out of committee. These were the general provisions of the bill as it reached the floor of the two houses of the legislature:

Two companies were authorized to build the road, the Union Pacific from the Missouri to the boundary of California; the Central Pacific from the navigable waters of the Sacramento or from near San Francisco to the border of California. (This was a triumph for Judah since he had pushed the organization of the Central Pacific Railroad Company and its incorporation so that the name could be in the bill.) If the Union Pacific reached the boundary of California first it could push on into California. If the Central Pacific got there first it could push on into Nevada. (Judah had insisted that his company should also incorporate in Nevada so that there would be no question of who would build the road in Nevada.)

The Central Pacific was granted a right of way through public lands of 200 feet on each side of the track and the right to take from adjacent land the earth, stone and timber needed for construction, but not the minerals. The company was granted every alternate section of land designated by odd numbers, to the amount of five alternate sections per mile on each side of the road within the limits of ten miles, but this land must not already have been sold, reserved, or otherwise disposed of by the United States and homesteaders were to be protected.

After the completion of each 40 consecutive miles on easy land and 20 on difficult land, three government commissioners were to examine the road and upon their certification patents should be issued covering the rights to the lands. Also upon the certification of the commissioners the Secretary of the Treasury was to issue the company United States bonds. This meant that the Central Pacific Railroad Company would have to build the first 40 miles with private capital before it could expect aid from the government. The financial subsidy was to amount to $16,-000 a mile where the building was easy, $32,000 a mile on high barren land between the mountain ranges and over the foot-hills and $48,000 a mile where the road crossed the mountains. Judah, who knew railroading as no other person on the committees could, had worked out these costs based on careful estimates.

In return for this support, which was expected to amount to about $50 million in bonds and about 20 million acres of land, the government would hold a first mortgage on the completed railroad and all its appurtenances.

Central Pacific was required to complete 50 miles of road in two years and 50 additional miles each year thereafter. The Union Pacific was to move twice as fast and the year 1874 was set as the last date of completion. One quarter of all bonds issued on the initial easy track and fifteen percent of those to be loaned on the section in between were to be withheld until the road was completed as a guarantee of completion.

When the act reached the legislators both senators and congressmen turned their minds away from the conduct of the war long enough to give it careful scrutiny. There was long debate with many of the debaters speaking from imagination rather than fact.

Many expressed doubts about the feasibility of the project. Lovejoy of Illinois said, "I do not believe the road will ever be built over the more difficult portions of the route." Campbell of Pennsylvania, a member of the House Select Committee, said, "It may be we cannot construct this road over the passes of the Sierra Nevada and the Rocky Mountains for the next fifteen years." William Tecumseh Sherman jeered, "A railroad to the Pacific? I would hate to buy tickets on it for my *grandchildren!*" Senator Collomer declared, "It will take a Samson to build this road, but this bill would give the office to a Samson without his beard [*sic*]."

Morril of Vermont thought that the road should be entirely a government enterprise: "There is no man in this house who doesn't know that if this road is ever to be built, completed and run, it is to be done by the Government of the United States. There is not a capitalist who will invest a dollar in it if he is to be responsible for its construction." And Senator Clark of New Hampshire expressed the same doubt: "I believe that if the

Good God were to make that road for you right through, you could not form a company in the country who could run it without failure."

But there were those who spoke out strongly for the railroad. Campbell of Pennsylvania, perhaps after a conference with Thaddeus Stevens who had an amendment up his sleeve, seemed to turn about and come back with renewed eloquence:

"This grand undertaking will do more to unite us as one people; will accomplish more by extending civilization over the continent — for commerce and civilization go hand in hand — than any other enterprise of modern times; civilization of that high type which shall spread to the cultivated valley, the peaceful village, the school house, and thronging cities through the mighty solitudes of the West; while the gold and grain of California and an intermediate continent flow in commingled tide to the marts of the Atlantic."

"If we could avoid the hazard of losing our Pacific possessions in case of war we must provide the means of defending them in only two ways," Phelps of California declared. "Either we must have a railroad across the continent by which munitions and troops can be readily transported to the coast, or we must maintain a sufficient force there in time of peace to meet the exigencies of war. To keep such a standing army on the coast for a few years only would equal the entire cost of constructing a first class road from the Mississippi to San Francisco . . . Two good reasons for passing the bill for this road: It is a military necessity, and it is essential to our internal development. Another reason, beyond the western terminus lie Japan, China and the East Indies with their more than 400,000,000 inhabitants whose commerce, the most tempting prize ever within the reach of any country, may be secured thereby. Not until we have completed a Pacific Railroad will this nation assume its proper position among nations."

And Aaron Sargent, without oratory, said succinctly: "The cost of land transportation of an army across this continent in time of peace is $20,000,000 and in times of war six times that much, $120,000,000. The journey across the plains six months or more, across the deserts, imposible."

At last the debate was ended. Thaddeus Stevens had unwrapped his amendment. All rails and other iron work was to be of American origin. This sounded good to the legislators and it pleased his constituents but it increased the cost of the railroad tremendously.

May 8, the House passed an enabling act 79 to 49. On June 20, the Senate passed a railroad bill thirty-five to five, and on June 24 the final bill passed the House. It was signed into law by President Abraham Lincoln just one day before the Army of the Potomac was forced to retreat to the James River. Judah had been in Washington seven months.

The directors of the Central Pacific Railroad Company waiting anxiously in Sacramento, received this telegram:

"We have drawn the elephant. Now let us see if we can harness him up."

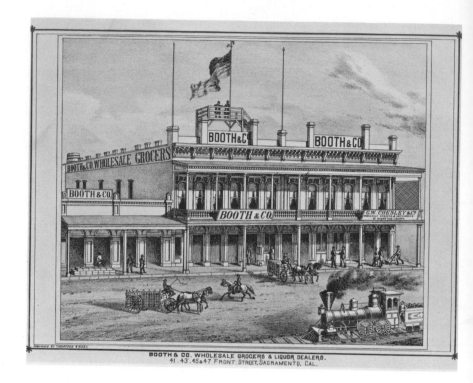

BOOTH & CO. WHOLESALE GROCERS & LIQUOR DEALERS.
41.43.45&47 FRONT STREET, SACRAMENTO, CAL.

Lucius A. Booth, the wholesale grocer who grew weary of
Judah's railroad talk, had his establishment on Front Street
where the first Central Pacific tracks were laid. From a lithograph in Thompson and West *History of Sacramento County.* —
HUNTINGTON LIBRARY, SAN MARINO, CALIFORNIA

TEN

It Takes More Than Talk to Build a Railroad

W HEN President Abraham Lincoln signed the railroad bill of 1862 Judah and Huntington did not stay in Washington to celebrate. Judah resigned from his positions on the railroad committees, closed forever the Central Pacific Railroad Museum, and took a hurried trip to see Anna. He knew that all of the careful work he had done in preparation for the presentation of the bill, all of his strength in the railroad committees, had won this brilliant success and he wanted to share the victory with Anna. Huntington felt certain that the bill would never have been passed if he had not "softened up" the legislators, used his considerable influence in its behalf.

Judah joined Huntington in New York and the two went railroad shopping together. Judah had estimated that the new railroad would need six locomotives, forty-two freight cars of assorted kinds and six first class coaches. He would also need to buy frogs, switches, turntables, track equipment and rails. He had decided on rails that weighed 60 pounds per yard, the heaviest available. These had been invented and first produced in England in 1855. Since all of the material would go by ship around the Horn it was necessary to purchase it at once.

Though Judah had not fully appreciated Huntington's "help" in Washington, feeling certain that he could have succeeded alone, his assistance when dealing with industrialists was of inestimable value. Judah's respect for Huntington grew when he saw him dealing with manufacturers on their own terms, when he found a wholesome respect for Huntington's credit among men who would have to begin the manufacturing of railroad material without an advance payment. In all of his hardware dealings Huntington had been scrupulously honest and had never allowed a bill to remain unpaid. Though Judah did not like Huntington and could never feel easy with him as he could with James Bailey or Daniel Strong, he did respect him.

One day Huntington called upon Oliver Ames and Sons, a firm he had done hardware business with. He coolly asked Ames for a loan of $200,000. "You mean to give bonds of something not yet in existence? I will have to look into this matter and think it over." The next day he said: "I have examined the books. I must say that no firm or customer that we have on our books has been more prompt in meeting their obligations in every way shape and form than the firm of Huntington-Hopkins during the time they have been dealing with us. Now do you intend to carry on the construction of this work in the same manner as you have carried on your business operations? Well, then, I do not hesitate to loan you the cash that you require. I will do this and take your bonds provided that Huntington and Hopkins take the same interest in the affairs of the road and look after my interests as they have done when I have sold them goods. I think I can be of more benefit to you in other ways than even loaning you money. I can give you letters to the different iron and locomotive men and others. I am acquainted with nearly all of them. I think these letters will be of advantage to you in making contacts with them."

First Judah and Huntington looked at locomotives. The locomotives were shining black decorated with scenes painted in brilliant colors. Sometimes they were even decorated with gold leaf. The manufacturers declared that the "art" work was essential to capture the female interest and trade.

"Nonsense," Huntington said flatly, which stemmed the flow of words. He wanted no "fancy" locomotives. He wanted them strictly useful. All he wanted to know is that they would hold up under hard work and a variety of weather conditions, that they would be strong enough to pull the necessary loaded cars up the steep grades. Judah, who had been interested in locomotives since his field trips with the older students at the Rensselaer Institute, was able to judge just how well each locomotive would function.

The two made purchases in New Jersey, Pennsylvania, and Massachusetts. It was not easy to buy any of the material they needed. The army was making an increasing demand for iron. So was the navy. Before the Civil War, vessels had been built of wood, but now the *Merrimac* and the *Monitor* had outmoded wooden ships. Every war ship had to be iron clad. While the railroad bill was still in committee the North had been shocked at the destruction of wooden vessels in Hampton Roads and had celebrated the *Monitor's* capability in making the Confederate ships retire.

With iron supplies so short that manufacturers could not guarantee the shipment of rails, and with plenty of iron rails available in England the reasonable thing would have been for Huntington to cross the Atlantic to buy the supplies he needed. Since all of the material would go by ship anyway, the extra shipping charge would more than be made up in the lower cost of materials. But Thaddeus Stevens had insisted on the amendment that provided that all material be of United States origin.

Judah had to select the material for which technical knowledge of design and structure was necessary; but when this work was completed he felt he was wasting time in New York when he might be starting construction in California. There was a great deal of work to be done before any of the iron was needed. Huntington could do the buying and bargaining for the company, at that he was excellent. He could be counted on to make every dollar count even in this seller's market.

Judah visited briefly in Greenfield and then he and Anna were once again on their way to Panama. On the steamer Judah spent much of his time in his stateroom working on careful reports to the directors of the company. His reports covered the preparation of the bill, its presentation in committee, its introduction on the floor of the House and of the Senate, the provisions of the bill and how they affected the company, and the purchases already made for the railroad. Anna watched with concern Theodore's feverish eagerness to use every minute profitably. She had thought that once the bill was through Congress he would rest; but resting was impossible to the driving nature of her husband.

In San Francisco and Sacramento Judah was met with great respect. No one called him "Crazy Judah" now. Everybody was eager to talk with him about his adventures in Washington. Word had reached California, probably though James Bailey, of how he had gained appointment to the important committees and had practically carried the bill on his own shoulders. This working himself into a position inside the committees was shrewdness that the young men of the West could appreciate.

Anna worried because Judah still talked of "my railroad," and in a very real sense it was his railroad since he had dreamed of it since his first appointment in California; he had tramped over every mountain pass in the central part of the state in search of a practical route; he had spent his winters in Washington trying to get a bill passed that would make building the railroad possible; he had used all of his own money and Anna's for the project. Every thought had been for the railroad, every minute he had worked to make it possible. But it was also Daniel Strong's railroad because he had been the man with the imagination to discover the possibilities of the Dutch Flat-Donner Pass route. It was, in a way, James Bailey's railroad, because he had given financial support to Judah when everybody else in Sacramento had thought of Judah's cause as "crazy," a support which at the time had been absolutely essential. And it was Huntington's railroad, and the railroad of the other men in the corporation because they had put up the money for the final survey and made possible the incorporation of the company named in the railroad bill.

When Judah presented his report to the board of directors he was astonished that some of the directors weren't satisfied with the bill and thought he should have done better. It was no use to try to explain to these men in quiet California what conditions were in Washington, throughout the North, really. Unless they had been in Washington themselves they couldn't possibly know how difficult it was, what an achievement it had been, to get a railroad bill before Congress at all.

"According to your report," Hopkins said, "the first 50 miles of railroad will cost $3,221,496."

"That is correct."

"According to the provisions of the bill 50 miles must be completed within two years and 40 of the 50 must be in use before any government money will be available."

"There will be state and county money," Judah insisted.

Hopkins' thin hand caressed his limp beard. "Three million dollars. We know what three million dollars are."

"We have excellent credit in the East. The bill will encourage capitalists to invest." Then Judah told of the reception that Huntington had received from the manufacturers. He knew that Hopkins was careful almost to a fault, that he had no daring for speculation, but still he was impatient with this dried-up man. Impatient and disappointed.

"Investors?" Hopkins asked. "Investors when you ask them to invest in a *second* mortgage with the government holding a first on everything?"

Judah left the meeting more than annoyed. At least Leland Stanford, the new Governor of the State of California, had congratulated him on his success. He felt he and Stanford would be able to work together well. Now he would leave the board of directors and the appointed commissioners to worry about money; he wanted to be at work in the field.

But Judah could not clear his mind of the human problems that pressed in upon him. L. L. Robinson, one of the men who had brought him to the West Coast and who had worked closely with him on the Sacramento Valley Railroad, wrote him a letter sizzling with anger. Unless the Central Pacific purchased Robinson's share of the Sacramento Valley Railroad upon his own terms, he would throw every obstacle in the way of the Central Pacific. He said that with the active opposition of his company, wielding a money influence of $30,000 a month, the Central Pacific could not hope to succeed and that he would wield that influence with all his power and energy against the Central Pacific both in California and in the East unless his terms were met.

SURVEYING FOR THE CENTRAL PACIFIC RAILROAD IN HUMBOLDT PASS.

One reads, "Judah made a careful survey through the mountains" and accepts the bit of information without recognizing what ingenuity, effort, even risk of life was entailed. This old line drawing appearing in *Harper's Weekly* is captioned, "Surveying for the Central Pacific Railroad in Humboldt Pass," says far more than words. Notice that even in a precarious job like this the men are wearing hats. — HUNTINGTON LIBRARY, SAN MARINO, CALIFORNIA

The letter, written in a rage to Judah, should have been written as a business proposition to the board of directors of the Central Pacific. Judah, with a single voice on the board of directors, could not have purchased the L. L. Robinson interest in the Sacramento Valley Railroad had he wanted to. He had a strong affection for the rails from Sacramento to Folsom. He had built this road and he was proud of its excellence. The transcontinental railroad could have begun at Folsom as well as at Sacramento. But Robinson's letter, with its threat, made reasonable negotiations impossible.

Anna, once again left alone in rented rooms, watched Judah go out with his surveying party. He explained to her that this was a different kind of survey. First, there had been exploration, then reconnaissance, next the careful preliminary survey for the making of estimates. The survey he was commencing now would be the last. It would establish the exact position of the road bed, the exact amount of fill and rock work needed, the exact line the completed road would follow over and through the treacherous mountains.

Back at work Judah could almost clear his mind of Hopkins' querulous questions, of L. L. Robinson's angry threats. This was the work he loved, the work he was certain that he had been born to do. Through the long golden autumn days he worked with his assistants under the sharp blue sky. He could feel the strength returning to his body and his spirit. The clear weather lasted into late fall. Fortune was indeed with him.

While Judah was out with his surveyors the Big Four developed a new scheme. In New York, in order to borrow money and to purchase materials on credit, Huntington had pledged not only his own personal fortune but the fortunes of Hopkins, Crocker and Stanford as well. In order to safeguard their fortunes it seemed to them that they couldn't wait for five years or more for the profits they expected to make when the road was finished. They were accustomed to doing business as merchants — quick turnover, quick profit. Judah, frequently in Sacramento for a few hours, had kept them informed about the progress of his survey and very soon, perhaps in January but certainly in February, grading would begin along the surveyed line. The Big Four saw that the contractors who built the road would make the first profits. Why not have these profits for themselves? During the months of October, November and December they met in each other's homes and made plans. These weren't board meetings. Booth, Marsh, Morse, Strong and Bailey were never invited to attend and even when Judah was in Sacramento at the time of the meetings he was not informed of what was going on.

Why not form a contracting company of their own to which they could let liberal contracts? A holding company that could undertake independent, quick money schemes like building a wagon road, going into the lumber business?

No, Leland Stanford said, neither would be honest. He was a slow, careful thinker, but once he had made up his mind he was adamant — or so he believed. This was business different from hardware or drygoods or groceries. He held out until the others convinced him that he ran the risk of losing his carefully accumulated fortune and then he wavered. Since Hopkins was the Central Pacific Treasurer all money matters could be handled "discreetly." Finally Stanford went along reluctantly.

By the time the autumn rains closed in, Judah had finished more than the surveying he had scheduled for the season. He returned to Sacramento and drew up careful specifications, accepted bids, investigated the contractors who had made the bids to be certain that each had the necessary man power and other facilities to do the work and was ready to present the contracts for the first section of the road at the regular meeting in December.

When Judah appeared at the meeting, the contracts ready for the board to approve, the associates were prepared for him. Before he had time to speak it was proposed that the contracts for the construction of the first seventeen miles of the road be let to the Charles Crocker Contracting Company. Judah was alert at once. He knew where the first profits were to be made and for members of the board of directors to take these themselves seemed to him to be a form of embezzlement. He jumped to his feet and spoke out against one of the board being given such a contract. Crocker, prepared for this outburst, rose and said jovially that he would resign from the board if it made Judah feel any better. He suggested that his place on the board be taken by his brother, E. B. Crocker, who was already the company's attorney. There was a quick motion to accept Charles's resignation and another to replace him with E. B., who happened to conveniently be present.

The whole thing was handled with such oily smoothness that it had obviously been planned if not rehearsed, and Judah and Bailey were alarmed. In a voice filled with passion, but still controlled, Judah explained that he had been building railroads since he was thirteen; that as chief engineer he had the right to handle the working contracts and oversee the work; that Charles Crocker, though an admirable man and no doubt able to handle other men, was not an experienced contractor. The friends of Charles Crocker listened to his words, then voted to give Charles Crocker the contract for the first 18 miles. He was to be paid $350,000 in cash, $10,000 in Central Pacific bonds, and $50,000 in company stock.

E. B. Crocker was brainy and cunning. Whatever he undertook he did with determination and he was determined that Charles should build the road, though Charles later admitted, "I could not have measured a cut any more than I could have flown." Judah looked at E. B., almost as big as Charlie, grayhaired, thin-bearded and falsely affable, and disliked and distrusted him. Just as determined as E. B., Judah resolved to fight the combine and have his way at least part of the time. All of the promises he had made the legislators and the people of California, all of the promises he had made the railroad committees and the legislators at Washington he had made in good faith and he was determined to keep his promises. He had built enough roads to know that if no locomotive ever crossed the continent, these scheming men could get rich from the government allotments he, himself, had engineered. It seemed to him that the very ideal he had spent his life for was being placed in jeopardy. There was one hope; that was that Charles Crocker might fail in doing the work for which he had no training or experience. Such a failure would be costly to the company, it might set the work back by months or even years while the Union Pacific pushed across Nevada. But if Crocker failed Judah would regain full responsibility.

These were the thoughts he expressed to Anna when, set-faced and heartsick, he told her of the meeting, the thoughts he expressed in an explosive letter to Daniel Strong who had not been present at the meeting.

The same heavy rains that had halted progress on Judah's survey drenched Sacramento during the latter part of December and on into January. On January 8, 1863, an unusually clear, balmy day, the Central Pacific Railroad Company and all of Sacramento celebrated ground-breaking ceremonies. A procession of carriages draped in bunting wound through streets hub-deep in mud. A temporary platform of new boards had been built on Front Street within a few yards of the flooded Sacramento River. Here the actual construction would begin. Two wagons filled with earth and draped with flags were drawn up near the platform. On one of the wagons was a banner showing two hands clasped across the continent from the Atlantic to the Pacific with the inscription "May the bond be eternal."

The platform was an island in a sea of mud. The procession stopped while bales of hay were dropped into the mud so the audience could stand on them and be saved the risk of being "sucked to China." Women in floor-sweeping skirts and gentle kid boots that could not be trusted in the mud, crowded the second floor balconies of the flat brick and wooden buildings of Front Street or remained in their carriages. Hardier women and most of the men and children pushed closer to the platform. A writer in the *San Francisco Bulletin* said: "If a man is going to be frightened by a little mud, he'd better go under a glass case at once and be set on the parlor table."

At a little after twelve the "notables" in frock coats, high silk hats and muddy boots climbed to the platform. Charlie Crocker, red-faced and jubilant, was the master of ceremonies. Technically he was nothing more than a stockholder in the railroad company, but the board of directors had given him a high sounding title, *General Superintendent of the Railroad*. He called the holiday crowd to order and introduced Reverend J. A. Benton, who offered an interminable invocation. Crocker then shouted, "The Governor of California, Leland Stanford, will now shovel the first earth of the great Pacific Railroad." Stanford took the shovel and without leaving the platform lifted it full of the soft earth waiting in the bunting-draped wagon.

Mural depicting the groundbreaking for the Central Pacific, hung in the Southern Pacific Sacramento station in 1931.— SOUTHERN PACIFIC COLLECTION (BELOW) A close-up view of the mural depicts the future and the past as well as the memorable day. Judah is at the right of the men on the speakers' platform. — CALIFORNIA STATE LIBRARY

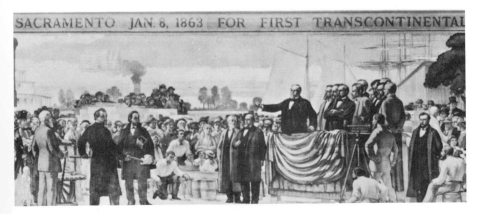

Nobody would have thought of descending from the platform and turning a shovelful of mud. The crowd cheered and a ten-piece band (paid for by the *Sacramento Union*) that had been waiting for this moment on the porch of the Exchange Hotel, struck up a tune. Crocker, growing more red-faced and bull-voiced by the minute, called for "nine hearty cheers." Men, women and children, especially children, complied with zest.

Then the "notables" settled gravely in to the business of the day. Stanford, who had gone to his own inaugural in a row boat since heavy rains often turned low-lying Sacramento into an American Venice, evidently didn't notice the mud or the fact that listeners were perched precariously on settling bales of hay. His speech had been carefully prepared and he didn't pro-pose to miss a word of it. In his slow, ponderous way he pro-mised the listeners that they would soon see "the busy denizens of two hemispheres in their constant travel over the great high-way of nations." Honorable A. M. Crane, President pro-tem of the Senate, promised: "Then will be celebrated the completion of this greatest, proudest achievement of man. Our sister city of the Bay will develop rapidly and by the amazing increase of her commerce and manufactures pass beyond any present conceived limits and sit proudly the Queen of Cities." A big promise to a city whose financiers had refused the opportunity of building the road. The people shifted on their hay bales. They cared little what happened to San Francisco.

There were five other speeches. Children cried, women lifted their skirts above their ankles to take them away from the invad-ing mud, men squirmed and shut their ears to the endless "speechifying."

Finally Crocker, all of his 250 pounds tense with enthusiasm, bellowed, "This is no idle ceremony; the pile driver is even now while I am talking, driving piles for the foundation of the bridge across the American River . . . It (the work) is going right on, Gentlemen, I assure you. All that I have — all of my own strength, intellect and energy is devoted to the building of the section which I have undertaken."

A shout went up, again the band blared, men helped women and children off the disappearing hay bales and into the car-riages. The second story balconies cleared, the carriages moved

AT THIS POINT
JANUARY 8, 1863
GROUND WAS BROKEN
INAUGURATING THE CONSTRUCTION
OF THE
CENTRAL PACIFIC RAILROAD
▲ ▲ ▲
THE WESTERN END
OF
THE PACIFIC RAILROAD
▲ ▲ ▲
THE FIRST TRANSCONTINENTAL ROAD
BANDING THE CONTINENT
WELDING THE ATLANTIC AND PACIFIC COASTS
AND
THE ONLY ONE BUILT FROM
THE PACIFIC COAST
EASTWARD
————— o —————
DEDICATED BY RETIRED EMPLOYEES
JANUARY 8, 1913.

Plaque marking the spot at Sacramento where ground was first broken for the Central Pacific Railroad on January 8, 1863. — SOUTHERN PACIFIC COLLECTION

147

off.

Huntington, in New York, was disgusted with the whole noisy affair. "If you want to jubilate go ahead and do it," he wrote. "These mountains look too ugly and I see too much work ahead. We may fail. There are many years of hard work between the beginning and the completion of this road."

Anna, in the Judahs' Sacramento rooms, felt hurt and puzzled. In all of the seven speeches no one had reminded the crowd that Theodore Judah had been talking railroad for eight years; that he had sought and received Congressional aid; that he had found the way through the seemingly impassable mountains. But when she spoke to Judah about this he didn't share her feelings. What was having been passed over in the celebration compared with the conviction that was growing relentlessly within him, though he still refused to admit it, that he wanted to build a railroad but the syndicate wanted to build fortunes. He spoke to her gently, "My dear, we set the ball rolling. Seven speeches and a shovelful of earth don't build a transcontinental railroad."

ELEVEN

Politics Moved Mountains

A S SOON AS THE contract for the first section of the
road was let to the Charles Crocker Contracting Company, Crocker sold his dry-goods business in Sacramento in order to give his full time to the railroad. The purchasers were men who had worked for him, even his competitors,
and when it was learned that he had sold at a loss Judah knew
that Crocker was serious about railroad building, that he was
in it to stay. But still there was the vague thought that Crocker
knew nothing about railroads and what he knew about handling
men would scarcely make up for his practical and technical
ignorance.

After the ground breaking, when actual construction began,
Judah was watchful. Charles Crocker was everywhere along the
construction area. In spite of his 250 pounds, and he was growing heavier every day, he was as agile as a boxer, welcoming
physical activity as if he had been starved for it. He was always
ready to lay aside his coat, pick up a shovel, and show a man
how the job was to be done. Judah had to admit that Crocker
was willing and that he knew how to work. But very soon
Crocker's real weakness became apparent. Not knowing anything about how to do the job he had sub-contracted it to several

149

contractors. Since these were sub-contractors, the men who took the contracts did not need to be passed on by the Central Pacific's board of directors. Crocker had not investigated the bidders to find out if they had horses or mules, carts and men at their disposal, or railroad know-how. It turned out that most of these sub-contractors had none of these necessities. They in turn sub-contracted to others who were as little able to cope with the problems as they had been.

Soon each major or minor firm that had a sub-contract or a sub-sub-contract was in the market bidding for horses and mules, trying to get hold of wagons and two-wheeled carts either by purchase or lease, trying to cajole men who were willing to work, from another contractor in order to build up its crews. All of this push for animals, vehicles, and men escalated the cost of everything and made for instability which Judah would never have tolerated. Riding along the route, he saw mound after mound of earth, some ten feet high, separated by untouched or barely scratched ground between. It would have been hard for most people to guess what the purpose of all these hillocks could be. Judah knew. Having studied the terrain carefully, he knew that the almost flat surface of this first "stretch" had top soil only a foot or two deep in most places. Under the top soil was a difficult-to-penetrate layer of gravel, hard sand and rock called concrete. The men, hired by the hour, moved the top soil. When they reached the concrete they moved on and put in their time moving more top soil. Most progress had been made not close to Sacramento, as it should have been, but near the end of the area since most of the workers were planning to continue with the pick and shovel only long enough to earn a stake and get off to the mines where fortunes might await them. They preferred to be nearer the mines when they quit work.

Judah knew that this whole mess was avoidable. Now was the time for him to sit back and watch Charles Crocker fail. But he couldn't do it. He couldn't watch the money that must be used to build the first 40 miles wasted with no road construction accomplished. As chief engineer he had the right to bring as much stability to the job as possible, to insist that the work that was done was purposeful and up to top standard.

So instead of allowing Charles Crocker to fail he kept at the job perpetually. Anna complained that he never rested; that sometimes he came in too tired to even undress for bed, but threw himself down for an hour or two of troubled sleep, then was back on the road again. With him always, he had his careful specifications. If a job had to be done several times and paid for several times too, it would be done right. The associates felt that he was too careful, that he was building too well. The difference was in point of view. He saw the first 40 miles of road as a part of a great transcontinental railroad that would someday bind all of the United States together — a road that would carry an untold number of passengers, an unpredictable amount of freight through uncounted decades. To the associates the first forty miles of road had to be good enough to pass government inspection, nothing more, so that government money would become available.

But there was one matter that all of the officers and directors were agreed upon. From somewhere they must get more money. The combined fortunes of all of the directors would not build the road, and the money that Huntington had raised in the East was readily exhausted. It was natural to turn to the State Legislature for State funds, to the county governments for additional money. Judah had counted on state funds when he defended the bill he had put through Congress at the time that the board of directors, particularly Hopkins, had objected to its provisions. Under pressure the State of California appropriated $200,000, which, of course, was far from sufficient to build the first forty miles. Judah had seen the Sacramento Valley Railroad so impoverished by interest payments that it had been unable to follow its original plans for expansion. Now Judah turned back to a plan that he had first had in Washington, a plan that he had formulated when he felt that the road should be built by private capital. He presented it at a board of directors meeting — such meetings were now almost a daily occurrence. The board should calculate the amount of bonds on which $200,000 would pay good interest. The amount was an amazing sum of a million and a half dollars!

Because of Judah's experience in working with legislators and because Leland Stanford was Governor of California, the state was induced to cooperate with the plan.

With guaranteed interest the purchase of stock seemed much less of a risk and the board of directors expected that investors would come flocking into the company. Even when Collis P. Huntington, the man who never made a mistake in a business deal, pushed the sale of stock, investors held back. Typical was the response of Commodore Garrison: "Huntington, the risk is too great, and the profit, if any, too small. We cannot take the risk." Judah must have been reminded of the reception his proposals had had in San Francisco before he had turned to the shopkeepers of Sacramento for support in organizing the company. Huntington personally called on most of the rich men in California, but purchases were few.

Surely sales would go better in the East. When Congress reconvened Huntington left for Washington. The Central Pacific Railroad Company wanted the United States to adopt a five-foot gauge so that it could use the already constructed California railroads as feeders to the continental line. Huntington would lobby for this gauge in Washington with the inside help of Congressman Aaron Sargent. He would also take time to visit the financiers of New York and Boston to peddle Company stock. Judah, who had lobbied for the railroad in three different sessions, was glad to see Huntington go. He would certainly be of more use in the East than in Sacramento. No one in the East called him "Old Huntington" as everyone did in Sacramento. He actually was an amazingly youthful man, straight, tall, lean but not thin, keen-eyed and knowing. He would represent the railroad well in the East. On this trip he took his wife, who had never been happy in California, with him. Rumor was that he was going to build a fine house for her in New York City, something she had never had in Sacramento.

In the East Huntington followed the pattern he had set in the West. He visited every wealthy man of his acquaintance. Much later he quoted one of them as saying, "Huntington, we do not want to go into it, but if you will guarantee the interest on these bonds for ten years we will take them." His reply was: "If the Central Pacific ever stops short of completion, C. P. Huntington will be so badly broken that you will never spend time picking him up."

To every man he called on he showed a letter from D. O.

Mills, a banker who knew each of the associates personally. The letter stated that Mills testified to the responsibility and honor of these men as men and as merchants, and whatever they agreed to do he believed they would faithfully carry out.

Huntington, selling himself as much as the Central Pacific Railroad, began to be successful in the East. At the same time Sacramento County pledged $400,000, Placer County $200,-000 and the city of San Francisco $600,000. The money the counties pledged was in bonds and was not available at the time the road was pushing the first few miles.

With the sale of bonds in the East money began to come into the hands of Hopkins. Though Judah was busy with his transit men and the completion of the working survey; although he was pushed beyond his physical limits checking the progressing work against his specifications, he wasn't blind to what was happening to this money. Costs exceeded estimates at every point. Charles Crocker was wasting a great deal of money while he learned as he went, and Judah spotted every error. He was not blind, either to the fact that Huntington, Hopkins and Stanford were silent partners of the Charles Crocker Contracting Company. His suspicions that the entire arrangement was a form of embezzlement were confirmed. Judah was not one to keep quiet under these conditions. At every board meeting he objected to the amount of money going to the Crocker Company. To avoid listening to Judah's objections most of the board meetings were held quietly in the home of one of the associates without Judah and his friends being invited. The only real board meetings were those set up in the by-laws which the associates couldn't avoid.

At one of these meetings the provisions of Judah's railroad bill were reviewed. The Central Pacific was to be paid $16,000 for each mile of road built on "easy ground," $32,000 for each mile through the foothills and $48,000 for each mile crossing the mountains. According to Judah's estimate this should be enough. True, he had underestimated the cost of the Sacramento Valley Railroad but he had been new in California then. Since that time experience had corrected his optimism. But the contract let to Charles Crocker Construction Company had been for almost $29,500 per mile, almost as much as the bill allowed

When the Central Pacific rails were laid this twelve miles of
track out of Sacramento, "up an imperceptible incline and without a single curve," shows that Judah was right about the foothills not beginning with the bank of the Sacramento River. —
HUNTINGTON LIBRARY, SAN MARINO, CALIFORNIA

for building through the foothills.

Then Leland Stanford spoke in his slow, thoughtful, ponderous way. "I believe we are building through the foothills. That every mile of our road is through the foothills."

"But that isn't true," Judah protested.

Governor Stanford remembered that in the book *Manual of Geology*, James Dwight Dana, the author, had said that the base of the Rocky Mountains began at the Mississippi River. Why didn't the base of the Sierra begin at the American or the Sacramento?

"They do not," Judah insisted. "I have surveyed and resurveyed every foot of that ground and there isn't even a perceptible rise." Then he accused Stanford of trying to move the mountains west to Sacramento. Well, said Governor Stanford, they would see what other experts had to say.

First Stanford asked for an opinion from Josiah W. Whitney, State Geologist, telling him first what he expected the opinion to be. On March 13, Whitney wrote a report in which he stated that at a point seven miles east of Sacramento began a "regular and continuous ascent." He also said that the rise was not "noticeable to the eye." Stanford then took the report to E. F. Beale, U.S. Surveyor General of California, and J. F. Houghton, the California Surveyor General, and asked them to concur in this opinion. Judah did not know what pressures or promises prompted these experts to make such a faulty decision. He did know that they all held their offices through political appointment.

When the opinion was presented to the board of directors Judah was enraged. To ask $32,000 a mile for building on this "slope" was robbery. He would not support any scheme to rob the government.

"We shall see if the government feels it is robbery," was the answer.

"President Lincoln will never consent to such a scheme," Judah declared. Although he did not know that Abraham Lincoln, who had never been West, would accept the report of "experts" and that A. A. Sargent would later wire, "Aaron's pertinacity and Abraham's faith has moved mountains," he went home bleak faced. These men, he now knew, would stop at nothing.

Pacing the floor of their small living room he told Anna, "I cannot make these men — some of them (Judah still had his supporters on the board) — appreciate the elephant they have on their shoulders. They won't do what I want and must do. We shall just as sure have trouble with Congress as the sun rises in the East if they go on in this way. They will not see it as it is. Something must be done."

Anna, seeing the weariness in Judah's face, replied only, "You are killing yourself, dear Ted. Killing yourself."

TWELVE

What About the
Dutch Flat Swindle?

W HILE Huntington was in the East the board of directors respected Judah as chief engineer. They knew nothing about railroad construction and they recognized their inability to make independent decisions. Judah wrote to Doctor Strong, "Leland Stanford is all right."

One of the changes in the original plan to which the board agreed was in the routing of the first mile of road. Huntington had wanted the road to go up I Street to Fifth, then across Fifth to B Street and out to the levee. (Later in reporting this incident he said, "I had *given orders* that the road should follow I Street to Fifth.") Judah thought the road should go up B Street rather than I. Building on B Street would take the tracks along the levee. Judah, having spent his youth in Troy, knew the value of a major wharf as a feeder for a railroad. The route would be more expensive to build than the one Huntington advocated, but it would have the advantage of being so close to the wharf that goods could be moved directly from ship to boxcar or from boxcar to ship.

Huntington returned to Sacramento on May 13. On a self-appointed inspection trip he came upon more than one hundred teams preparing railroad grade along the levee.

"Stop this work at once," he ordered.

The teamsters and laborers had their orders from Judah; they hesitated to take an order from anyone else. Huntington's way was so dictatorial that one of the men ran to find Judah.

When Judah came back with the man Huntington thundered, "What do you mean building the road on B Street when it should be going up I Street? Building this near the river will mean using expensive rip-rap."

Holding his temper with difficulty, and unwilling to make a scene before the working men, Judah answered quietly, "The board reconsidered the route in your absence. It was decided that the advantages outweighed the disadvantage of added expense."

Huntington replied with the tightening of the thin lips that Judah had grown to hate. "It will cost $200,000 at least to put the road here. It must go up I Street." Then he turned to the foreman and said, "Mr. Cody, shift your men. This road will go up I Street."

Judah stood his ground and protested Huntington's interference with the actual engineering of the road. "You are but one member of the board of directors and I am the chief engineer."

Huntington didn't even raise his voice. "There will be no work done on this road until it goes up I Street."

The road went up I Street.

Huntington had also come back to Sacramento with the idea of pushing the building of a wagon road. This, Huntington said, was not to be just for the purpose of carrying men and materials for the railroad, but it should be an excellent, well-surfaced toll road that would capture the trade between Sacramento and the Nevada mines.

"Why, you can have a wagon road if not a railroad, "Judah had promised Huntington and his associates. He had also said of the projected railroad: "It is purely local; you are tradesmen in Sacramento City; your property, your business is here. Help me to make the survey. I will make you the company. And with the (railroad) bill passed you will have control of business interests that will make your fortune in trade if nothing more."

Not many teamsters saw the magnificent scenery of the rugged Sierra range as the wagons plodded along the narrow wagon road. — HUNTINGTON LIBRARY, SAN MARINO, CALIFORNIA

Teams travelled nose to headgate on the wagon road as it wound through the Sierra. — HUNTINGTON LIBRARY, SAN MARINO, CALIFORNIA

A wagon road through the Sierra was no mean project. This portion of the road photographed at the foot of Crested Peak was hacked out of solid rock. — HUNTINGTON LIBRARY, SAN MARINO, CALIFORNIA

Those had been his promises at the first meeting ,and now, he felt, the situation had changed completely. When Huntington had insisted on resurveying all of the possible routes before beginning work on the Dutch Flat-Donner Pass route, Judah had urged that instead of spending the time and money on these unnecessary surveys it would be better to begin a wagon road that could carry men and supplies to the railroad work site. Now, when the Railroad Bill had been passed by Congress providing for assistance in money and land, when the counties and the city of San Francisco had voted bonds to help build the railroad, the time for building a wagon road had passed.

The associates used Judah's own arguments in favor of a wagon road. It was essential to the building of the railroad, Judah had said. He still felt that a wagon road that served this one purpose was necessary; but not the toll road Huntington had in mind. He declared that if the railroad were being constructed mile by mile out of Sacramento instead of in bits and pieces men and supplies could be carried to the work site on the railroad. Huntington reminded him that the rails, purchased in the East, would not be delivered for months. Probably not even then since Confederate privateers were busy on the sea lanes. Even if the road bed had been graded as Judah had wanted it to be there could be no rails laid soon enough to transport men and supplies.

It wasn't until August 1863, that the Wagon Road Company was incorporated with the purpose of "constructing and completing and maintaining a wagon road and collecting compensation for the use thereof over the Sierra Mountains from Dutch Flat to Washoe Valley . . . with such extensions and branches as the said company shall determine." Owning stock in the Wagon Road Company were, besides the Big Four, E. J. Bradley and Daniel W. Strong. But work had been going on for some time before the incorporation.

Judah appreciated the logic of their arguments in favor of the wagon road — the arguments had been his not so long ago — but what made him furious was that he knew the associates weren't really thinking of the best good of the railroad. What they had in mind was seizing control of freight and passenger service from Sacramento to the mines. The proposed road, connecting Dutch Flat with Carson Valley near Virginia City, certainly could be no help to the railroad. But the railroad completed as far as Dutch Flat could be a help to the wagon road.

Most of the money for the road building came from the Big Four; Judah thought he knew where it was really coming from. It had been raised in the East to build the railroad, been paid to the Charles Crocker Contracting Company for doing very little, and much of it had been returned to the private money bags of the associates. The money that would build the wagon road, Judah knew, was money that should be going into the railroad in order to build the first forty miles without government assistance.

Judah made allowances for his friend Doctor Strong. What Daniel Strong had wanted from the first was the wagon road. Even though he gave up his railroad holdings for Wagon Road stock he and Judah remained close friends.

The building of the toll road would, of course, be contracted to the Charles Crocker Contracting Company. The Wagon Road Company could buy ready built a long section of toll road over which supplies and "fancy goods" were moving to Virginia City where every man had more money than he could spend. The associates decided to buy that road, add it to their own projected road and capture part of the freight carried by the Sacramento Valley Railroad. When the Central Pacific was completed to Dutch Flat the associates would carry all of the trade. Judah had been astonished and hurt when the Sacramento Valley Railroad had dismissed him as chief engineer, he had been angered by L. L. Robinson's threatening letter, still he hated to watch the associates plan to make the Sacramento Valley Railroad useless.

Judah suspected that the associates had two ambitions: First, to get to Dutch Flat — for this he was responsible in part at least; second, to acquire the government subsidies and add as much of them as posible to their private fortune. For this he was responsible, too, in a way, since the subsidies were the result of his long continued, self-sacrificing efforts in Washington. Nothing was turning out as he had planned. He had not foreseen that Huntington, the son of a tinker who had clawed his way to financial success, would be incapable of unselfish action or that he would be able to carry his associates with him.

People not associated with the Central Pacific Railroad, watching the Associates at work, saw that the group's major interest was to get to Dutch Flat as quickly as possible. The San Francisco newspapers accused the Central Pacific Railroad of planning to build only to Dutch Flat to connect with the wagon road. They headlined their articles and the broadsides they distributed all over the area, THE DUTCH FLAT SWINDLE. The *Alta California* of San Francisco said: "The Sacramentans are determined to have no railroad but Dutch Flat. The Capital City has aided in the raid upon this county of $800,000, upon Placer County for $25,000 and upon the state for millions, all for the benefit of that scheme. It will yet prove its ruin. There will never be a railroad via Dutch Flat to Nevada Territory. There are obstacles which cannot be overcome. The Pacific Railroad will follow another route, not through Sacramento or anywhere in the vicinity."

The people who read the newspapers and the broadsides couldn't know that this prophecy would prove completely false; they could only feel cheated and angry. Judah was blamed as much as the others—probably more because the public thought of him as Mr. Central Pacific — though he fought consistently and vigorously for what he knew to be best for the railroad and the people it would serve. He fought against the associates turning their interest from the railroad to the wagon road. He fought against the awarding of contracts to the Charles Crocker Contracting Company. He refused to close his eyes to the money that went from the Pacific Railroad Company to the Crocker Contracting Company and back to the money bags of the associates. His frustration was expressed in this letter to Doctor Strong:

"I had a blow out about two weeks ago, and freed my mind, so much so that I looked for instant decapitation. I called things by their right names and invited war; but council of peace prevailed and my head is still on; my hands are tied, however. We have no meetings of the board nowadays except the regular monthly meeting, which, however, has not been held this month; but there have been a quantity of private conferences to which I have not been invited. I cannot tell you what is going

THE GREAT

DUTCH FLAT

SWINDLE!!

The City of San Francisco

DEMANDS JUSTICE!!

THE MATTER IN CONTROVERSY, AND THE PRESENT STATE OF THE QUESTION.

AN ADDRESS

To the Board of Supervisors, Officers and People of San Francisco.

Title page of a pamphlet warning the public that they had been promised a railroad but would get only a wagon road to Dutch Flat. — MARINERS MUSEUM

Title page of a pamphlet warning the public that they had
been promised a railroad but would get only a wagon road
to Dutch Flat. — MARINERS MUSEUM

on . . . suffice it to say that I have had a pretty hard row to hoe. I try to think it is all for the best, and devote myself with additional energy to my legitimate portion of the enterprise."

And he did devote himself completely to his work. He and his assistant, Lewis M. Clement, worked at the railroad office every night until after midnight. They were making estimates of the costs of repair shops and other buildings that would be needed when the railroad was in operation. He urged the board of directors to continue the railroad survey across Nevada so when the time came to build there, the final survey would have been completed. The associates were too interested in their wagon road.

The meetings in the homes of Stanford, Crocker, Huntington and Hopkins became more frequent. Judah knew that they were planning some major move. But the move they decided upon was incredible.

Hopkins called a special meeting of the board. He demanded that each stockholder pay in full for his stock before the stock could be listed. While the move was within the law it crowded out all of the small stockholders and the associates were able to purchase the stock for a small percentage of its face value. The board now consisted of the Associates, Huntington, Stanford, Hopkins and E. B. Crocker sitting in for his brother, Charles, and on the other side Judah and his loyal friend, James Bailey. Judah was comfortable. His stock was paid for in full by his seven years of service to the railroad before the formation of the Company.

But Hopkins' next move was to demand that Judah pay at least ten percent of the cost of the stock he held. Why? The stock had been paid for in full. Anna had been concerned about the verbal agreement but Huntington had said that was the way business was done in Sacramento and that was the way he wanted it. Bailey advised Judah to "hold out."

Another sober meeting of the board of directors was called. The money from the sale of bonds in the East was exhausted. The road had not been completed for 40 miles — far from it. The grading wasn't even finished. Not a single shipment of track had yet arrived in California. The government money would not be available for no one knew how long. It was true

166

that county and San Francisco money would soon be available, but there was nothing in the treasury to go on with the work.

Judah talked of the "Pacific Road." He and Bailey suggested that the Company mortgage the section of the road that was graded and all of the equipment. Huntington, usually coolly controlled, retorted in anger, "No, let's not talk about a Pacific Road. Don't spread yourselves. Let's go slow and steady and own what we build." Judah tried to project his vision beyond Dutch Flat and made an impassioned plea for the mortgage that would save the railroad from being forgotten. Huntington answered, "I never build castles in the air."

Judah had always built dream upon dream.

"A mortgage will ruin our personal as well as our joint credit," the financiers objected.

"It could be lifted with county money that will be available very soon," Judah insisted.

"Not soon enough," they said.

And then they unveiled the idea they had been working on in their private meetings. What they wanted to do was to reach an agreement that the directors of the company share equally (not according to the amount of stock each one held since the associates had bought out the small investors, but equally) in the cost of the work until the county money became available.

This was the end. This was the pinch the associates had planned. They knew that Judah could not share equally with them. He had the knowledge, the dedication to build the road, but not money. His money and Anna's had been spent in those trips to Washington through which he had finally succeeded in procuring the Railroad Bill of 1862; for the years when he was preparing exhibits, profiles, estimates that would prove the road feasible; for the Railroad Convention. "Crazy Judah," "Mr. Central Pacific," Theodore Dehone Judah, engineer and railroad builder, since he couldn't raise money equal to the contribution of the others would no longer be a part of the road which for more than seven years he had thought of as "my little road." James Bailey could have written a check for the amount he would owe if the measure passed the board, but he voted with Judah against the associates. The measure was passed over their vote and Bailey refused to pay. Now James Bailey and Collis P. Hunting-

167

ton faced each other across the table. Huntington was furious at the opposition, though for some time they had been planning to "unload" Bailey. "Bailey, I'll buy you out or you will buy me out. Which will it be?" "I'm not selling or buying," Bailey answered shortly. Huntington's voice rose to an unaccustomed shout. "Then there's only one alternative. The work must stop at once." He left the meeting, mounted his horse and rode off. By nine o'clock all of the grading on the road had stopped and Huntington was back in Sacramento. "I'll give you two weeks to raise the money to buy me out," Huntington told Bailey.

James Bailey was determined to accept Huntington's challenge. He started at once to contact every wealthy man he knew on both the East and the West Coast. With the help of the transcontinental telegraph he was able to make contacts that a short time before would have been impossible. For two weeks not a shovel full of earth was lifted. All along the right-of-way dirt heaps were abandoned. Judah, riding the length of the project, saw dirty children playing on one of them. "I am the King of the Coconut Tree," one of them called out continuously pushing every other boy who tried to climb to the top down its crumbling sides. Huntington was like this boy, maintaining his position by pushing others down — a despot. But Bailey would climb to the top. He'd buy Huntington out and the Coconut Tree would have no king.

Within two weeks Bailey found a buyer, Charles McLaughlin of Boston. Judah was jubilant when he heard the news. With Huntington out of the syndicate he could build the railroad as he knew it should be built. He could raise the money in a manner he thought was ethical and use it honestly to the best of his ability. He put his worries and troubles behind him. Anyone had to admit that Huntington had been useful, especially in purchasing materials in the East, but a wealthy man in Boston would do this just as well.

"Whose interest am I buying?" McLaughlin asked when it came time to close the deal.

"Collis P. Huntington is selling out."

McLaughlin wired, "If Old Huntington is going to sell out, I am not going in. Just what sends him out will keep me out."

So James Bailey, who had financed Judah through the early reconnaissance of the Sierra, who had gone East with him and Anna when the time had come for a showdown with Congress, who, with Judah, had stood out against the avaricious dealings of the associates and who from the first had shared Judah's dream, was forced out. His position as board secretary was taken by a former business partner of Hopkins; a man so accustomed to "little" business that his books show such items as "glue 25 cents, carrying wood 37 cents, desk eraser 50 cents."

With Bailey gone Judah's position, which had been difficult before, became untenable. On one side of the table were the Big Four, Huntington, Hopkins, Stanford and Crocker, and on the other, standing alone, "The first of the Giants," Judah.

Rail and river transportation at Sacramento circa 1869.
Taken from the deck of a river packet, this photograph
shows a wharf brig lying between the steamer and the
piling of the levee. Up the river are a scow schooner and
three sloops. All freight cars on the right carry the Central
Pacific herald. — ROBERT WEINSTEIN COLLECTION

THIRTEEN

The Final Struggle
for Control

ANNA, WATCHING Judah's tired face, worry-darkened eyes and sagging shoulders, could only guess what was happening on the road and in the railroad office. She knew that Huntington and her husband had never agreed. How could they? They were so very different. Huntington was born in a shanty, put out to support himself while he was still a child, taught by hard knock after hard knock to be crafty and ruthless in taking care of his own interests. Judah was an aristocrat, born in an Episcopalian manse, married into a prominent "solid" family. Huntington had turned hardware and blasting powder into a fortune and Judah had turned everything that he was or could hope to be toward the fulfillment of a dream.

Anna knew that Huntington had refused Judah's plan for a railway building; that he, without any engineering experience or education, had changed an item in Judah's estimate of the first careful survey of the Dutch Flat-Donner route; that he had so little confidence in Judah's ability that he had insisted on a long and expensive resurveying of four other routes; that he had over-ridden the decision of Judah and the board of directors to take the road up Sacramento's B Street. These differences were common knowledge. She knew, too, how Judah felt about

the Charles Crocker Contracting Company and the liberal contracts turned over to it; about how the associates were trying to
move the mountains to seven miles east of Sacramento; about
how the associates had "unloaded" James Bailey and squeezed
out the small stockholders. Yet she couldn't even imagine the
daily indignities to which he was subjected. Whenever she spoke
to Judah about his troubles he assumed a false optimism to
protect her.

Yet he worked overtime every day getting his part of the enterprise in running order, preparing his assistant to take over.
All of his own time he spent in writing letters. Many of these
were to Daniel Strong.

On July 10 he wrote: "I have had a big row and fight on the
contract question and although I had to fight alone, carried
my point and prevented a certain gentleman from becoming a
further contractor on the Central Pacific Railroad at present."
And in the same letter: "Huntington seems to possess more than
usual influence . . . Stanford, who I told you was all right, is as
much under their influence as ever . . . The wagon road seems
to be a tie which unites them, and its influence seems to be paramount to everything else . . . They have been consulting and
looking over the way every day, and do not hesitate to talk
boldly, openly, before me, but not to me, about it. They talk as
though there was nobody in the world but themselves who
could build a wagon road . . ."

But most of the letters were written to acquaintances in the
East. He was nursing a scheme to bring Eastern investors into
the Pacific Railroad to buy out Huntington and his associates
who seemed to him to be so inadequate to understand the problems of a transcontinental road, so eager to make money at its
expense. He may have written to Vanderbilt who was interested
in increasing his holdings in the West. He may have written to
George Francis Train of Boston who had already shown his enthusiasm for the transcontinental railroad. Or perhaps he wrote
to Dr. Durrant and his associates who were interested in the
Eastern end of the line. There were certainly others, but since
his move could not be publicized and still be effective, the
names do not appear even in Judah's intimate letters to Doctor
Strong.

The board of directors meeting on July 1, 1863, was a momentous one. Judah reported: "Section 19-31 inclusive, or from the line of the California Central Railroad, have been let to responsible contractors and will be commenced immediately." The "row and fight" Judah mentioned in his letter to Doctor Strong probably was over the acceptance of this report. But on this same day the other directors voted to pay him $25,000 worth of Central Pacific stock for his "service as agent in the Atlantic States and prior to the organization of the company." Three days later they issued $66,000 worth of additional stock, bringing to $91,000 his payment in stock. The verbal agreement when the company had been incorporated had been for $100,000 in stock for these services.

All through July and August Judah hung on, completing his correspondence with the financiers in the East. In September he sold his Nevada Rail Road stock to Crocker, probably for cash to support his effort to find new financiers to take over the company. At the time James Bailey sold his Nevada Rail Road stock to Asa Philip Stanford, Leland Stanford's younger brother.

Early in October Anna once again packed the right gaiters. Since Judah planned to be back on the Coast in December she may have packed little else. Anna wrote much later that Judah had told her that "he had secured the right and the power to buy out the men opposed to him and the true interests of the railroad . . ." and that ". . . everything was arranged for a meeting in New York City on his arrival. Gentlemen from New York and Boston were ready to take their (the associates) places."

It is difficult to guess just what arrangements Judah had made with the Big Four before he left Sacramento. Huntington said in 1890 that Judah was paid $100,000 for his interests. He may have referred to the payment in stock since Leland Stanford said under oath that Judah's position with the company was unchanged. "He had not been dismissed from his position with the Central Pacific Railroad Company nor had he disposed of his interests therein." Probably he made an agreement with the associates that if he could find interested financiers in the East he would buy each of them out or if he failed in his attempt they could buy him out. The amount set for each purchase may have been $100,000.

Congressman John C. Burch, who had shared Judah's optimism for the railroad since 1859 when they had sailed together on the S. S. *Sonora,* said that Judah intended to combine his capital with a great deal more which he had already "lined up." "The plans were fully matured, his coadjuters selected, and meetings arranged. Judah's scheme was to buy the Central Pacific Railroad and place its management in the hands of a new set of men of known public spirit who would, without other designs to hinder or obstruct them, prosecute diligently the main work of completing the railway from ocean to ocean."

Why did the Big Four make such an agreement with Judah? They had watched Bailey and Judah fail in getting enough capital together to buy out just one of them. They may have thought that getting enough together to buy out all four would be impossible and Judah would be brought to understand that his place in the railroad was to be just chief engineer and nothing more. Then, too, they were more interested in their wagon road than in the railroad and while it was only partly finished it was already bringing in fabulous returns.

On October 3, 1863, Judah and Anna once more boarded a ship for Panama. While the S. S. *St. Louis* was still in San Francisco Bay Judah wrote this letter to Dr. Strong:

"I have a feeling of relief in being away from the scenes of contention and strife which it has been my lot to experience for the past year, and to know that the responsibilities of events, so far as regards the Pacific Railroad, do not rest on my shoulders. If the parties who now manage, hold the same opinion three months hence that they do now, there will be radical change in the management of the Pacific Railroad, and it will pass into the hands of men of experience and capital. If they do not they may hold the reins for a while, but they will rue the day that they ever embarked on the Pacific Railroad.

"If they treat me well they may expect a similar treatment at my hands. If not, I am able to play my hand. If I succeed in inducing the parties I expect to see to return with me to California, I shall likely return the latter part of December."

Judah really did relax as they travelled south, though his brain buzzed with his plans to interest Eastern capitalists in the transcontinental project. His correspondence with them had been so favorable that he was almost certain of success. One night he roused himself from his bunk to say to Anna: "Anna, what can I not do in New York now! I have always had to set my brains and will too much against other men's money. Now, with money — equal — what can I not do!"

Before the S. S. *St. Louis* reached Panama it passed the *Herald of the Morning* sailing northward. The *Herald of the Morning* had rounded the Cape carrying 100 tons of rails for the Central Pacific Railroad.

As Theodore and Anna and the rest of the passengers of the S. S. *St. Louis* crossed the Isthmus of Panama in a coughing little train, the sky blackened. When they arrived in Aspinwall torrential rains were falling. Passengers clung to the protection of the little train. Judah braved the deluge to buy a big umbrella. With the umbrella he escorted women and children from the train to the ship that would carry them north. Seeing women waiting in the protection of hotel doorways he escorted them, too. Anna knew how tired he was and that he was doing too much. She begged him to stop his gallantry and come in from the near-cloudburst. He replied, "Why, I must do this, even as I would have someone do for you. It is only humanity."

When all of the passengers were safely on board he went to his stateroom and put on the dry clothes Anna had waiting for him. Still he was cold. When Anna saw him shivering she begged him to go to bed and get warm under blankets.

"Anna, I have a terrible headache," he admitted, and willingly got into bed.

Anna, thoroughly alarmed, called the ship's doctor to their stateroom. He examined Judah, almost casually it seemed to Anna, then turned to her and said, "Your husband has yellow fever." Yellow fever, dreaded, almost always fatal, yellow fever! There was little the doctor could do to make Judah comfortable, nothing he could do to arrest the illness. The stateroom was quarantined, and Anna was alone with her husband. For eight days she watched beside him, never undressing, never allowing herself more than a few minutes sleep at a time. She bathed his face with cool water, held his hand, soothed him. He was delirious and talked of nothing but "my road."

At the New York wharf, some time on October 26, the ship's

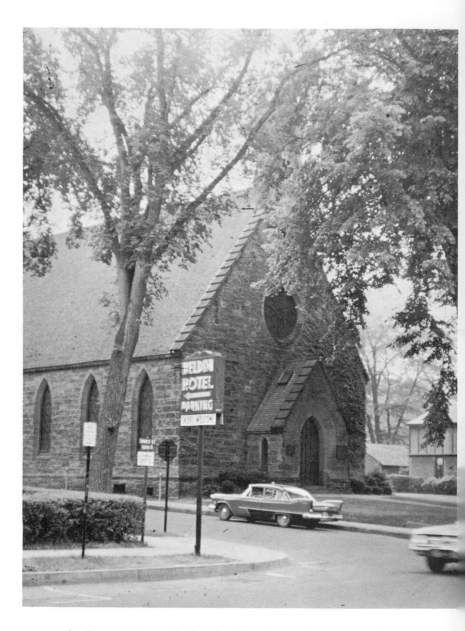

St. James Episcopal Church. Theodore and Anna Judah were
the first to be married in this quiet stone church in Greenfield.
An eagle lectern still in use was the Pierce family memorial to
Theodore. — ROBERT WEST HOWARD

"He rests from his labors" doesn't seem as fitting an epitaph for hard driving Theodore Judah as some other line might be. In choosing the epitaph Anna no doubt had in mind the last frustrating year of his life. "We started the ball rolling," might have been his own choice. (BELOW) It was here that Anna celebrated the completion of the transcontinental railroad, alone with the spirit of her husband. — BOTH ROBERT WEST HOWARD

doctor helped to carry Judah to a carriage and Anna took him at once to the Metropolitan Hotel where they had reserved rooms. She sent the hotel porter with a message to Dr. F. N. Otis, a family friend. He hurried to the hotel and looked at Judah whose face was a livid yellow, his lips foam flecked; he put his arm around Anna's shoulders and said as gently as possible, "Anna, dear, it is yellow fever. Ted is dying of yellow fever."

Now that Anna had someone to lean upon, her reserve broke. She insisted that he was too young to die, that his life work was still before him, that he must recover to fulfill his dream.

"Ted is dying, Anna. He has been overworked. Worn out. Such men fall victim to this fever."

On October 30, just four days after the first rails were laid on Front Street in Sacramento, Anna and Dr. Otis knelt in prayer beside Judah's bed. As they prayed Judah mumbled again, " . . . the road . . ." "Anna, we started the ball rolling" had been the end of the sentence in all of his almost incoherent mumbling but now he said only, ". . . the road . . ."

He died at dawn on the second of November. In four months he would have been thirty-eight.

Anna took his body by Connecticut Valley Railroad to Greenfield for burial in a quiet cemetery "not a stone's throw from the old home where I (Anna) had always lived."

Three days later his death was front page news in Sacramento. It was incredible. Incredible. To the people of Sacramento the Central Pacific Railroad and Theodore Judah were inseparably connected.

And in the meeting of the board of directors the Big Four passed a resolution of sympathy" for the widow" and advanced Samuel Sherry Montague to the position of chief engineer.

FOURTEEN

The Central Pacific
Reaches Promontory

PERHAPS IT WAS with a feeling of relief that the directors of the Central Pacific passed a resolution of sympathy for Judah's widow. Now they could "go it alone," setting their own policy and building immense private fortunes as well as a railroad. Leland Stanford would handle the political strategy, Collis P. Huntington would stay in the East purchasing material and getting money, Mark Hopkins would see that a good part of the money landed in the bank accounts of the Big Four, and Crocker would establish a record for actual work seldom equalled in the history of America. Theodore Judah had done two heroic things for which his associates would never forgive him. He had recognized the Charles Crocker Company as a means of making money for Crocker and his silent partners even if the railroad was never completed, and he had stood firmly against the legerdemain that had moved the foothills to within seven miles of Sacramento.

In the next phase of the Central Pacific Railroad Charles Crocker, ruthless as he was, "vain, boastful, stubborn, tactless, bull-like" as his contemporaries called him, emerged as sort of a hero. Many years later Crocker told his son, "If it becomes necessary to jump off the dock in the service of the company

179

J. H. Strobridge "Stro" was friend and confident of Crocker. In the field, like Crocker, he pushed the men to the limit of their endurance. — SOUTHERN PACIFIC COLLECTION

instead of saying, 'Go, boys,' you must pull off your coat and say, 'Come, boys,' and let them follow you." His dedication of his enormous body and even more colossal will to this principle of leadership made possible the building of the railroad.

Samuel Sperry Montague, who took Judah's place, was an excellent engineer, hardworking and highly skilled but lacking in Judah's genius. He was willing to be an engineer only and take orders rather than trying to be the conscience of the builders, so he suited the Big Four perfectly. He tried in vain to better Judah's carefully drawn plans and specifications.

Crocker needed help on the job and he found a "straw boss" who was almost a double of himself in James H. Strobridge. "Stro" could use his fists just as effectively, curse just as loudly and endure just as much brutal work and privation as Crocker. He became not only the construction boss, but Crocker's closest friend.

In building the first 18 miles over easy terrain Crocker and his silent partners made $425,000; this was all of the track that was completed in 1863. In 1864 he built twelve miles more. The wagon road, undertaken by the associates in 1863, was finished June 14, 1864. It developed a business of a million dollars a year "with freight teams in an unbroken line three and four miles long at a stretch." So why hurry with the railroad? Besides railroad money had run out.

The locomotive *Governor Stanford* turned out by Richard Norris & Sons of Lancaster, Pennsylvania, had arrived in Sacramento March 10, 1863. It was shipped unassembled and put together in Sacramento. On its first run guests drank to the memory of "T. D. Judah, late Engineer of the Pacific Railroad." By 1865 it hauled freight and passengers 30 of the miles required by the railroad act that Judah had pushed through Congress. But still, before subsidies could be received from the government, ten more miles of track must be laid. Had Judah been allowed to correct Charles Crocker's costly mistakes as Crocker learned railroad construction, had he been allowed to issue competitive contracts, had he been able to handle all of the money that had been available to the company, the money spent would have been more than was needed to build the forty miles and no pause in the work would have been necessary. There was noth-

An early passenger train with flat roofed coaches crosses the
Newcastle trestle on its way to end-of-track. — ROBERT WEIN-
STEIN COLLECTION (BELOW) Chinese workers with picks and
shovels, chisels and hammers, one-horse dump carts and black
powder carve their way through and over the granite reaches
of the Sierra. — SOUTHERN PACIFIC COLLECTION

ing wrong with the railroad bill of 1862, but with the men who insisted on building private fortunes with government money.

July 2, 1864, President Lincoln signed a new railroad bill that doubled the subsidies granted in 1862 and at the same time permitted the companies to issue first mortgage bonds which would take precedence over the bonds of the United States, making it a first mortage and the lien of the government a second mortgage. The same law fixed the subsidy for the first 150 miles across the Sierra Nevada at $48,000 per mile and for the 600 miles across the desert at $32,000 per mile. Senator Wilson had said, "I would sink $100,000,000 to build the road and think I had done a great thing for my country. What are $100,000,000 in opening a railroad across the central region of this continent that shall connect the people of the Atlantic and Pacific and bind us together?"

These millions looked pretty big to Crocker and his associates. Early in 1865 Crocker, with all of the money he needed provided by the 1864 railroad bill, began to push ahead at a surprising rate. He had learned much in the two years he had been working on the road and he was a man who grew with experience. By March he had reached Illinoistown, blasting, clearing forests, dumping fill. By the end of May the railroad was 56 miles long and earning more than $1,000 a day hauling passengers at ten cents a mile and freight at 15 cents a mile for each ton.

Everything looked more than promising until Crocker ran out of labor. It was the same problem that had beset the builders since the first, but now it was made more difficult because the road was closer to the mines and anyone employed to work on the road and carried to the site of construction was likely to head for either the Comstock or Nevada Territory. Twelve-year-old boys were hired by the company.

It was Stanford and Crocker's brother who suggested that the road hire Chinese. Several thousand Chinese were already in California working as laundrymen, gardeners and house boys, or scratching and rescratching the already worked-over gravel pits hoping to find gold. Crocker thought the idea splendid and when Strobridge protested he said, "They built the Great Wall of China, didn't they? That was almost as tough a job as this railroad, wasn't it?" Crocker hired fifty Chinese, stacked them

Chinese laborers were let
down in buckets to chisel
away at the granite cliffs.
— JOHN GARMANY COLLECTION

into flatcars and carried them to the point of operations. The
Chinese pitched their camp, cooked their rice, went to bed and
the next morning were ready for work. The salary was $26 a
month.

Stro seemed to have a secret hope that they would collapse
under the work so he could say, "What did I tell you?" but after
twelve hours of backbreaking labor they were still working at
top speed. A hundred more Chinese were hired in the next two
days and by the middle of summer, 1865, there were 2,000 working on the road. Now Crocker had several thousand brought
by ship from China, contracting to ship their bodies back to
China to be buried with their ancestors should they die in
America. By the beginning of 1866 there were 6,000 of "Crocker's Pets" working with picks and shovels on the granite slopes.
Here the work was practically impossible but the Chinee did it,
hanging like wall-walking flies to the face of the cliffs, carring a
70 pound sack of blasting powder at each end of a shoulder pole.
No one knows how many of these tenacious, uncomplaining
workers were killed in building on the mountains and no one
seemed to care. On pay day Charles Crocker, "Chollie Clocker"

Many legends have grown up around the exploitation of the
Chinese laborers on the Central Pacific. It is true that the
Central Pacific could never have been built without them. —

to the Chinese, rode his mare past the waiting men. In one
saddle bag he had silver, in the other, gold, and he paid each
man in coin as he read their names from his list. This was Crocker's way of working and his son said that his father never slept
in his Sacramento bed in his fabulous new Sacramento home
more than three successive nights for six years. He preferred to
be on the job, planning and pushing and bellowing and accumu-
lating a fortune.

"Everyone was afraid of me. I was just looking for someone
to find fault with all the time. My faculty for leadership grew
more and more," Crocker later wrote.

Then the real mountains were reached. Judah had been
acquainted with these mountains and had described the hard-
ness of the rock, the steepness of the grades, the number of
tunnels that must be built, the gorges that must be filled. But
Crocker, fully occupied with the work wherever he was, had not
studied Judah's specifications.

Cape Horn was a sheer granite cliff which Crocker could
not go through or over. Judah had planned that the road would
go around it, so around it Crocker went, lowering the Chinese

on ropes to pick out a ledge wide enough for other workmen to stand on to make the cut wide enough for the road. Now the railroad passed through Dutch Flat and pushed on beyond giving the lie to those who had cried, "Dutch Flat Swindle." By November another 28 miles of track were completed. Fifteen thousand Chinese were working on the road and $8,000,000 had been spent.

Stro, just behind Crocker, was grading roadbed and laying track. He was working just as tirelessly as Crocker. Now they both faced the problem of building fifteen tunnels through rock so hard that picks and chisels, even blasting powder, were useless. A Swedish chemist analyzed the rock and developed T.N.T. trinitrotoluene that was more effective. In one explosion Stro lost an eye. In another a whole Chinese crew was blown to bits and Crocker was unable to keep his contract to ship the dead back to lie by their fathers.

Summit Tunnel was built at the rate of eight inches a day through the marble spine of the mountain. Chinese worked at both ends and a shaft was driven straight down in the middle so other crews could work from the middle toward the ends. This quarter-mile tunnel is the most expensive bit of railroad in all of railroad history. It is characteristic of Crocker, with his contempt for things he did not understand, to have refused to try a newly invented steam drill.

More and more the Big Four, especially Huntington and Stanford, were concerned about the progress of the Union Pacific westward. According to the act of Congress, each road could go as far as it was able to until it met the other. Building across the desert would be easy and therefore rewarding. While Crocker's Pets risked their lives building the road through the Sierra Summit, the Union Pacific, working on prairie, pushed hundreds of miles westward.

The winter of 1866-67 was so severe that work became impossible. Avalanches buried whole work crews, whose bodies would not be seen again until spring. Fifteen feet of snow covered the frozen ground. Crocker pushed on 24 miles, from Cisco to Donner Lake, but then he had to give up and ship the freezing Chinese back to Sacramento until the weather changed. Samuel Sperry Montague with his transit crews on sleds, started

186

Judah had forseen the need for the Summit
Tunnel. It was built eight inches a day
through the marble spine of the mountain. —
HUNTINGTON LIBRARY, SAN MARINO, CALIF.

work in the Truckee River Canyon. As soon as the spring opened
up the Chinese were back, 15,000 of them, the largest work
crew that had ever been assembled in America. The spring
thaws washed the earth out from under the tracks as if the road
beds had been made of sugar, and Stro had much of his work to
do over, but the rails pushed on. Now Crocker was building as
well as Judah had planned to build.

The winter of 1867-68 was as severe as that of '66-67. Again the
Chinese were sent back to Sacramento while Crocker, Montague
and Strobridge erected a sawmill and with white mechanics
and laborers felled the trees, shaped the lumber and built 37
miles of snow shed to protect the workmen busy on the road
and later the finished rails and the trains that ran over them.
"Railroading in a barn" this was called, but there were no more
crews wiped out by avalanches. In June of '68 the road over the
summit was completed and the tracks that had been laid on the
western side of the Sierra were joined to those that had been
laid to the Nevada line. To cross California had cost $23,000,000.

Now the race was on to cross the Nevada desert, the Union Pacific eyeing the desert with the same appetite for money that the Central Pacific had shown. "Every mile built meant a profit of twice its cost." Huntington on the East Coast was working as hard as Crocker in the West buying necessary material, arranging for bottoms to ship it on. There were 39 of these ships on the way around the Horn at the same time.

In vain Judah had begged the Big Four to push the survey into Nevada. Now Montague was using several crews to do the work that might have already been completed. The surveyed line through Nevada twisted and turned to make the longest route possible and to avoid any terrain that would have to be prepared before road bed could be constructed. Judah would never have allowed a survey like this. Crocker's Pets had their wages raised from $26 to $35 a month when the temperature rose to 120 degrees.

Now a new labor force entered the railroad picture. The Mormons with their settlements in Utah, under the direction of their president, Brigham Young, had already entered into a road-building contract with the Union Pacific to build the road from Echo Canyon west to Ogden. The Mormon road building arrangements were different from any that had ever been made in America or elsewhere. Brigham Young entered into the contract, then subcontracted to John Sharp, his own son, Joseph A. Young, and Joseph F. Nounan. These were all capable men. These men then subcontracted to "companies" formed either from one ecclesiastical unit (called a ward) or from a group of wards. Each group of men elected its own president, who acted as foreman, and went to work. Sometimes they willingly turned over their wage credit to their ward for such work as building a school or a chapel. Sometimes, if they were recent immigrants, they paid their wages directly to the "Perpetual Emigration Fund," a loan fund established by the Mormon Church to bring new converts to the United States and overland to Utah.

This looked like a good source of labor and management to Leland Stanford, who spent a good deal of time in Utah getting acquainted with "Brother Brigham." In the fall of 1868 Brigham Young entered into a contract with Leland Stanford in the

"Building in a barn" people said when snow sheds were built to protect the completed road during the winter. Miles of such sheds were erected in the Donner Pass region. — HUNTINGTON LIBRARY, SAN MARINO, CALIFORNIA (BELOW) An Indian at the top of the Palisades in Nevada gazes down on the Central Pacific tracks. — ROBERT WEINSTEIN COLLECTION

Tough as he was, Strobridge couldn't live away from his wife
and family so they went with him. Sometimes they lived in a
car at end-of-track. (BELOW) There was no rowdiness in the
Chinese camp. The tired men ate their rice and retired. —

names of Ezra T. Benson, Lorin Farr and Chauncey W. West. The Mormons were to build 200 miles of Central Pacific road for $4,000,000.

With these work crews there was no swearing, no drinking, no gambling, no work on Sunday. Painstakingly, feeling the honor of the Church and the Territory at stake, they did their work.

Why Brigham Young entered into these contracts is easily explained. This is from a letter to a Church publication in England:

"For many reasons that will readily occur to you, this contract is viewed by the brethren of understanding as a Godsend. There is much indebtedness among the people, and the Territory is drained of money, but labor here and coming we have in large amount, and this contract affords opportunity for turning that labor into money with which those here can pay each other, and import needed machinery, and such useful articles as we cannot yet produce, and those coming can pay their indebtedness and have ready means with which to gather around them the comforts of life in their new homes.

"It will obviate the necessity of some few thousand of strangers being brought here to mix and interfere with the settlers, of that class of men who take pleasure in making disturbance wherever they go. It will give the money expended in the work to citizens of this Territory and work to employ them, which is very desirable at the present time. It will show that we are interested in forwarding the great national project and ready to assist in consumating this great national good."

With the Mormons grading from Echo Canyon to Ogden (150 miles) and from Humboldt Wells, Nevada, to Ogden (200 miles), Charles Crocker, Strobridge and the others could concentrate on the completion of the rest of their roads. Both sides were so eager to push the greatest distance that surveying crews were setting up lines almost side by side and grading crews were grading roads that paralleled each other for miles.

In Congress both Huntington of the Central Pacific and General Dodge of the Union Pacific were lobbying strenuously to get the point of joining the rails as far from their starting points as possible. Finally Promontory Summit, 53 miles west of Ogden, "the most desolate place on God's earth," was chosen. Later Ogden was to become the railroad town of the Rocky Mountain West. This made little difference to either company since both companies wanted the subsidies for completed miles and these were counted from Promontory. Besides, both companies had received an unexpected bonus when the Mormon Church donated all of the land for railroad roundhouses, car barns and station.

Quickly five saloons were erected at Promontory to be ready for the celebration that would accompany the completion of the road and a few opportunists set up other attractions on the dismal flats.

At last the road was finished; this part of Theodore Judah's dream had come true. The historian Hittell says:

"There were no troubles encountered except what had been fully seen and appreciated and set forth by Theodore Judah in his original surveys. There were no harder rocks to be drilled, than he had stated, no steeper grades to overcome than he had measured, no more extensive or difficult cuts, fills, or tunnels than he had described."

Over Theodore Judah's route and the twisting snake-like desert route of Montague the trains would run, and Judah's part of the route would stand to this day as the best possible route over the Sierra Nevada.

FIFTEEN

The Golden Spike

O
N THE DAY the Central Pacific was to be joined with
the Union Pacific the raw little town of Promontory in
Northern Utah was crowded with celebrants.

Governor Leland Stanford and his guests, California Justice
Sanderson, Governor Safford of Arizona, three federal commissioners and several friends had arrived from Sacramento on
May 7, in time for the celebration to be held May 8, in spite of
an unexpected incident. The special train had left Sacramento
as the second section of the regular morning train at 6:30 A. M.
behind the locomotive *Antelope*. As the train steamed down
the Truckee River grade, Dr. W. H. Harkness, wrapped in a
buffalo robe and riding on the pilot to see all that there was to
see for his paper, *The Sacramento Press*, saw an enormous log
rolling toward the tracks and recognized that the locomotive and
the log would reach the same place at the same time. Chinese
workmen felling logs to feed the ever hungry wood-burners,
had seen the morning train go by and had thought the way was
clear. Dr. Harkness didn't stop to consider the wisest course.
He jumped. When the log, 50 feet long and three feet in diameter, struck the *Antelope* the locomotive was badly damaged,
but it limped into Reno. There a wire was dispatched to Wads-

worth to hold up the first section. At Wadsworth the special cars were coupled to the regular section behind the locomotive *Jupiter*, and pulled into Elko. Since most of the passengers were disembarking at Elko to go to the adjacent mines, the regular train was left there and the *Jupiter* went on to Promontory drawing only a water car and Stanford's two private cars.

Mark Hopkins and his guests arrived on another special. All of the Central Pacific officials who would be present at the wedding of the roads were on time for the May 8 celebration.

The Union Pacific was not so prompt. The train carrying the officials would not arrive until Monday. The reason given was that there had been a wash out on the line; though perhaps the real reason was that when the special reached Piedmont, 83 miles west of Green River, the unpaid workers refused to let the train through until they had received their wages. The payroll had to come by wire from Omaha, which meant a delay.

The celebrations in Sacramento and San Francisco had been planned for Saturday and the delay at Promontory didn't change the plans.

Governor Stanford and the others made a short sight-seeing trip into Mormon Utah and then the *Jupiter* took the special train back to the tip of the Great Salt Lake where they waited until Monday morning.

Monday morning was clear and though the date was May 10, so cold that the sticky white clay was covered with a thin sheet of ice. According to the plan the two special trains would arrive from the East and from the West at the same time and the citizens of Promontory were out early so as not to miss anything. Everybody raised a good natured jeer when construction trains loaded with graders, track layers, and teamsters drew in before the ceremonial engines. The Governor's train had been shunted to a siding to allow the construction train to pass.

At noon the official cars from the West were drawn into Promontory. At one o'clock Stanford left his car and joined Hopkins and the other officials at the point where the last rail was to be laid, the last spike driven. The screech of the Union Pacific whistle was heard and a great shout went up from the crowd. The Union Pacific officials left their train and joined those from the West. There were vice president Thomas C. Durant; Major-

President Stanford's train, powered by the *Jupiter,* on its way
to Promontory passes Monument Point, May 8, 1869. (BELOW)
Strobridge's special train stands at the end-of-track at Promontory early on the morning of May 10, 1869. — BOTH ROBERT
WEINSTEIN COLLECTION

General Grenville M. Dodge and Colonel Silas Seymour. This was the same Silas Seymour who had advised his brother Horatio, Governor of New York, to recommend Judah as the chief engineer for the Sacramento Valley Railroad. Judah had not only engineered the Sacramento Valley Railroad but had been the real moving force in making the Central Pacific possible. Perhaps Silas Seymour was the only man who had had an active influence on both parts of the transcontinental road. There were others on the Union Pacific Directors Car: superintendent Samuel Reed, Sydney Dillon, John Duff, the Casement brothers. Following the official train was a trainload of officers and men, several companies of the 21st infantry and a regimental band on their way to the Presidio in San Francisco.

Soldiers, turned policemen, kept back the crowds and made room for the photographers. Such a crowd! Irish and Chinese laborers, teamsters, cooks, train crews, engineers, railroad officials and their guests, sightseers from California and Salt Lake City. Many of those from the East and from the West had hoped to see the fabulous Brigham Young but the Mormon Church's president and prophet had sent Bishop John Sharp, called the Railroad Bishop, and Colonel Savage to represent him.

The band played, a picked group of Chinese laborers dressed in spotless denim pantaloons and jackets and with their hair neatly braided and tied in pigtails trotted out carrying the last rail. From the Union Pacific side came a work force carrying a polished laurel tie which they quickly placed. With everything in readiness for the driving of the last spike work was halted while a Massachusetts pastor offered an invocation. The telegraph operator finally announced, "We have got done praying; the spike is about to be presented."

There wasn't just one spike but several. Each was presented with oratory and dropped into a hole provided for it: one of Comstock gold from Nevada Territory, one of an alloy of gold, silver and iron from Arizona Territory; a silver and gold spike from Idaho and one from Montana, and finally two gold spikes from California. Dr. Harkness, evidently recovered from his leap from the tender of the *Antelope* presented the last spike to Leland Stanford. It was an unusual spike, twice as long as the usual spike. David Hewes of San Francisco had had W. T. Gar-

196

At the moment of the invocation, photographer Russell captured this scene from the cab roof of Union Pacific No. 119. (BELOW) Russell's famous picture of the Golden Spike ceremony. Years later Governor Stanford commissioned an artist to reproduce the scene. It now hangs in the California State Capitol in Sacramento, and painted into the picture are many men who were not at the ceremony, including T. D. Judah, deceased for four years. — BOTH ROBERT WEINSTEIN COLLECTION

THE GOLDEN SPIKE
On the head of the last spike was inscribed the legend "The Last
Spike." — SOUTHERN PACIFIC COLLECTION

ratt, also of San Francisco, melt down 18 twenty-dollar gold
pieces and form them into this spike. Schultz and Fisher, also
of San Francisco, had engraved it. The piece broken off was
later made into rings, tiny bells, watch-fob spikes for the men
who had assisted most in the actual building of the road.

Stanford placed the spike in its hole, lifted the silver hammer
with which he was to tap it in place, struck — and missed. This
wasn't an insignificant miss since when the hammer touched
the spike the spike would touch a telegraph wire leading to the
hole and the telegraphic signal would drop a ball from above
the capitol dome at Washington announcing the completion
of the transcontinnental road and setting off the ringing of
church bells throughout the United States. A boy had been sent
shinning up a telegraph post to secure the connection between
the ground wire and the telegraph wires.

When Governor Stanford missed the spike an impatient tele-
grapher touched the key to set off the planned cycle. Vice president Durant stepped up and tried his hand with the silver hammer. The spike was driven in and the road was completed. "My
country 'tis of thee / Sweet land of liberty / Of thee I sing."
The Twenty-first Infantry Band played and in spite of the mud

Andrew J. Russell's wet plate of "East and West Shaking Hands at the Last Rail." — AMERICAN GEOGRAPHICAL SOCIETY

and the mishaps a thrill swept the five hundred onlookers that made the throat grow tight and the eyes wet.

The two engines moved slowly over the newly laid rails. When they touched cowcatchers the engineers drank champagne from the neck of the same bottle. Now the engine from the East ran onto the Western track, backed up and allowed the Central Pacific's Jupiter to come forward on to the Union Pacific track. The wedding was over and it was time for the real celebration. Workmen drew out the valuable spikes and replaced them with hardier ones, the officials from both lines went first to the private car of vice president Durant to help him to frame the telegram to be sent to President U.S. Grant, then to the private car of Leland Stanford. The workmen and the sightseers moved into improvised bars for their own celebrations.

During the celebration in Governor Stanford's car, workboss Strobridge brought in the Chinese director of all the Chinese laborers that had worked on the Central Pacific and the little man, symbol of the part the Chinese had played in building the Western railroad, was given a standing ovation. But all the day long there had been no mention of Theodore Dehone Judah,

Judah who was "crazy" enough to have made the whole road possible.

In Greenfield, Massachussets, Anna celebrated. In the white frame house of her brother "not a stone's throw from the cemetery" she sat alone. She had refused to receive guests, not because she was hurt at not having been invited to the celebration, but because she wanted to spend the day alone with her memories of Judah and of the dream they had shared. The young surveyor, brightest of all the young men who were building railroads in the Northeast, who had asked for her hand in marriage and had been given it . . . The brilliant young engineer who had accomplished the impossible feat of building the Niagara span, doing much of his work from their honeymoon cottage overlooking the falls . . . The pioneer railroad man of the West who had taken her away from everything that was dear and familiar . . . The jubilant young man who, with three others, had ridden a handcar on the first rails to be laid in California . . . "Crazy Judah" who alone had pushed the building of this railroad . . . Those sweet days when they had picnicked on the slopes and hiked up the canyons of the Sierra, Judah with his barometer and she with her sketch pad . . . The months she had spent in Greenfield reading his terse letters from Washington . . . the museum . . . the lobbying . . . the work on special "inside" committees . . . Judah's joy at the incorporation of the Central Pacific with shrewd business men to back him in building the road and the year of contention that had worn him out for the attack of fever on the Isthmus . . . The "alone" years when she had followed the course of both railroads, hearing in spite of herself of the pyramiding fortunes of the builders who had behaved as Judah had feared that they would.

But now the church bells were ringing and it was time to go. She put on her hat, wrapped her shawl around her slender shoulders and walked alone to the cemetery to share with Judah this hour of completion of their dream. It was three o'clock, and twenty-two years before at three o'clock she and Judah had been married.

"It seemed," she wrote, "the spirit of my brave husband descended on me, and together we were there . . ."

Bibliography

ORIGINAL SOURCES

Reminiscences of Charles F. Crocker	Bancroft Library, University of California at Berkeley.
Reminiscences of Collis P. Huntington	Bancroft Library, University of California at Berkeley.
Reminiscences of Anna P. Judah	Bancroft Library, University of California at Berkeley.
Hopkins-Huntington Letters	Timothy Hopkins Transportation Library, Manuscript Department, Stanford University Libraries.
Hopkins, Timothy, Random Notes on Central Pacific History	Timothy Hopkins Transportation Library, Manuscript Department, Stanford University Libraries.
Stanford, Leland, Letters	The Leland Stanford Papers, University Archives, Stanford University Libraries.
Telegram Copies, Central Pacific	The Leland Stanford Papers, University Archives, Stanford University Libraries.

RAILROAD DOCUMENTS

Report of the Chief Engineer of the Sacramento Valley Railroad, 1854.

Report of the Chief Engineer of the California Central Railroad, 1858.

Pacific Railroad Convention. Report of Theodore D. Judah, accredited agent Pacific Railroad Convention upon his Operations in the Atlantic States, August, 1860.

Report of the President, Trustee and Superintendent of the Sacramento Valley Railroad, Feb. 1, 1861.

Report of the Chief Engineer of the Central Pacific Railroad Company of California on his Operations in the Atlantic States, 1862.

Pacific Railroad Act of 1862.

SPECIAL SECONDARY SOURCES

Burch, John C. *Theodore D. Judah.* First Annual of the Territorial Pioneers of California, 1877.

Wheat, Carl I. *A Sketch of the Life of Theodore D. Judah.* California Historical Quarterly, Vol. IV. September, 1925.

SELECTED SECONDARY SOURCES

Bancroft H. H. *History of California,* San Francisco, California, 1888.

Bancroft, H. H. *Chronicles of the Builders of the Commonwealth,* San Francisco, California. The History Company, 1891.

Bowels, Samuel. *Across the Continent.* Springfield, Mass. Samuel Bowles and Company, 1865.

Carr, Sarah Pratt. *The Iron Way.* Chicago, Ill., A. C. McClurg and Co., 1907.

Cleland, Robert Glass. *A History of California; The American Period.* New York, New York. The MacMillan Company, 1923.

Evans, Corinda. *Collins Potter Huntington* (volume 2). Newport News, Virginia. The Mariners' Museum, 1954.

Fulton, Robert Lardin. *Epic of the Overland.* San Francisco, Cal. A. M. Robertson, 1924.

Goodwin, C. C. *As I Remember Them.* Salt Lake City, Utah, 1913.

Griswold, Wesley S., *A Work of Giants.* New York, Toronto, London. McGraw Hill, 1962.

Holbrook, Stewart H., *The Story of American Railroads.* New York, New York. Crown Publishers, 1947.

Kneiss, Gilbert. *Bonanza Railroads*. Stanford, California. Stanford University Press, 1941.

Lewis, Oscar. *The Big Four*. New York, New York. Alfred A. Knopf, 1938.

Perkins, J. R. *Trails, Rails and War*. Indianapolis, Indiana. Bobbs Merrill Company, 1929.

Quiett, Glen Chesney. *They Built the West*. New York, New York. Appleton Century Company, 1934.

Rae, W. F. *Westward by Rail*. London. Longman Green and Company, 1871.

Reed, G. Walter. *History of Sacramento County*. Los Angeles, California. Historic Record Company, 1923.

Russell, Charles Edward. *Stories of the Great Railroads*. Chicago, Ill. Charles H. Kerr and Company, 1912.

Sabin, Edwin L. *Building the Pacific Railway*. Philadelphia, Pa. J. B. Lippincott Company, 1919.

Shuck, Oscar T. *Representative and Leading Men of the Pacific*. San Francisco, California. Bacon and Company, 1870.

Walker, David H. *Pioneers of Prosperity*. San Francisco, California, 1895.

Young, John P. San Francisco: *A History of the Pacific Coast Metropolis*, Chicago, Ill. S. J. Clarke Publishing Company, 1912.

NEWSPAPERS (1856 to 1869 *passim*)

Alta California, San Francisco, California
Bee, Sacramento, California
Bulletin, San Francisco, California
Deseret News, Salt Lake City, Utah
Journal, Nevada City, California
Journal, San Francisco, California
Signal, Auburn, California
Tribune, Salt Lake City, Utah
Union, Sacramento, California

Acknowledgments

No one writes a book like *Rails from the West; a Biography of Theodore Judah* without the unselfish assistance of countless people. There are writers who have recorded their research in published books; there are libraries and archives where original manuscripts, long out of print documents and pictures taken more than a hundred years ago are available. A complete acknowledgment would be impossible.

I wish to particularly express appreciation to the Association of American Railroads, the Bancroft Library, the California Historical Society, the California State Library (California Section), the Huntington Library and Art Gallery, the Mariners' Museum, the New York Historical Society, the Rensselaer Polytechnic Institute, Pasadena Public Library, the Stanford Libraries, the Society of California Pioneers and the Southern Pacific Company (Public Relations Department).

Dr. Leonard Arrington of Utah State University and Dr. Edwin H. Carpenter, Western Americana Bibliographer at the Huntington Library, read the manuscript and made helpful suggestions. Mr. Allen R. Ottley, California Section librarian of the California State Library and Mrs. Dolores W. Bryant, research librarian of The Society of California Pioneers, gave me far more help than I could have reasonably requested. Mrs. Hazel G. Pray, Historian of the Greenfield Massachusetts Historical Society and Miss Gladys Pierce, niece of Anna Pierce Judah, corresponded with me regarding little known information about Mrs. Judah and furnished previously unpublished pictures. Gerald M. Best, railroad historian, directed me to little known newspaper material. My husband, Ivan Jones, has been patient with me during the five years I have been working on the book, taking me wherever material was available, following Judah's route over the Sierra and finally proofreading the manuscript.

Index

Hall, A. W., 9

Harper, Widow. — Faces grading teams with shot gun, 23

Hopkins, Mark — Fire losses, 21; described, 97-99; critical of railroad bill, 139; crowds out small stockholders, 166;

Huntington, Collis P. — Fire losses, 21; present at first meeting, 94; calls meeting at Prentice home, agrees to carry survey through, 95; calls second meeting, 97; described, 104-108, subcribes to C.P.R.R., 109; rejects Judah's plan for a railroad building, III; works with federal legislators, 129; shops for rails, locomotives, etc., 135-137; argues for 5 foot gage; seeks further financing, 153; changes route through Sacramento, 157-158; pushes building of wagon road, 158.

Johnston, Albert, Sydney, 124

Judah, Anna Pierce — Meets Judah in Greenfield, 11; prepares exhibit for convention, 63; active at convention, 65; suggests railroad museum in Washington, 69; celebrates Golden Spike alone, 200.

Judah, Theodore Dehone — Recommended for California post, 9; goes to New York conference, 12; accepts position, 15; foretells his part in transcontinental railroad, 17; arrives in San Francisco, 19; maps plan to measure railroad business and sets up office in Sacramento,21; completes preliminary survey for S.V.R.R., 22; estimates cost, 24; begins laying of rails and takes first ride, 27; envisions the transcontinental railway, 29; promotes survey from Sacramento to Benicia, 41-42; explores the Sierra for pass, 43; surveys a wagon road, 44; decides to go to Washington, 45; promotes federal survey of central route, 49; writes *Practical Plan for Building the Pacific Railroad*, 49-51; plans a Pacific railroad convention, 53; chief engineer of California Central 55; appointed by railroad convention to carry memorial to Congress, 66; continues search for Sierra mountain pass, 81; reaches Donner Summit, 84; barely escapes death, 86; dismissed from S.V.R.R., 88; presents opportunity for railroad investments in San Francisco, 90; engineering decisions questioned, 115; explores Feather River route, 116; makes estimates on Donner Pass route, 116-117; reports to board of directors, 117; accredited agent of C.P.R.C. to Washington, 119; urges incorporation of C.P.R.C. in Nevada, 121; secretary of Senate Committee on Pacific Railroad, 127; Clerk of House Committee, 127-129; resolves to fight the Big Four, 143; not mentioned in ground breaking ceremonies, 148; criticized for working too well, 151; developes a new plan for financing, 151; unable to raise personal assessment, 167; decision to bring in Eastern investors, 172; sold his Nevada stock, 173; conceives plan to gain control of the C.P.R.C. 173; takes ship for Panama 174; plans for the future expressed to Dr. Strong, 174; becomes ill in Panama, 175; dies in New York, 178;

Knights of the Golden Circle — Active in California, 123; Active in Southern California, 124.

Latham, Milton — Proslavery, 123; Favored railroad, 127.

Lincoln, Abraham — Signed railroad bill of 1862; Signed railroad bill of '64, 183.

Logan, John A. — Conference with Judah, arranges for Pacific Railroad Museum, 73.

Locomotives — *Antelope* scheduled for Promontory celebration, 193. The *C.K. Garrison,* earlier the elephant, 33. *Governor Stanford* arrives in Sacramento, 181. *Jupiter* at the Golden Spike celebration, 194. *Nevada* arrived from Boston, 83; trouble on way to Folsom, 35. *L.L. Robinson,* arrived from New Jersey, 33. *Sacramento,* first locomotive unloaded, 27; takes celebrants to Folsom, 35-37.

Marshal, James, 13

McClellan, General George — Replaces Winfield Scott, 124; refuses to move, 127

Mills, Robert, 45

Montague, Samuel, Sperry — Puts transit crews in Truckee River Canyon, 187; built snowsheds, 187; Survey crews into Nevada, 188.

Mormon Church — Entered into railroad contracts, 188; road building arrangements, 189; condition of work, 191; donates land for round house, etc., 192.

Morse, 27

Moss, J. Mora, 29

Nevada Railroad Company. Incorporated, 122

Nicaragua. — Vanderbuilts route to Pacific, 18; macadam road, 19.

Noble Pass, 64

Ogden, Utah, 192

Pony Express, 77

Promontory, Utah — Meeting of Union Pacific and Central Pacific, 192; Golden Spike celebration, 193-200.

Railroad Convention — Called, 60; convened, 65.

Railroads East of Mississippi — Buffalo, New York & Erie, 11; Chicago, Burlington & Quincy, 74; Chicago & Rock Island, 74; Connecticut Valley, 9; Erie Canal 9, 11; New Haven, Hartford & Springfield, 9; Schenectady & Troy, 9.